Cwmbra

CW01501554

Hollybush

The location of the Hollybush Inn accoı number 4 Two Locks Road.

The earliest mention of it in the census records was in 1861 where it was referred to as the Old Bush Inn. The head of the house at this time was a widow named Elizabeth Pugh. She was sixty-two years old and a laundress from Liverpool. Living with her was her son George, aged thirty-one, who worked as a forge labourer. Elizabeth's daughter. Julia, aged seventeen, was a harpist.

There is no mention on the census of the property being used as a public house however by the time of the 1871 census Elizabeth had changed her occupation to that of a beer house keeper. Her family had grown to include three grandchildren – Julia, eighteen, George, fourteen and Clara, nine.

The Pugh family had left the Hollybush Inn before the year 1878 as it was recorded in the South Wales Daily News of 23rd March as being for sale. It's tenant at this time was Jesse Sadler. The property was described as 'desirable, in first class condition and admirably located for business'. We can gain a brief description of it from this report – 'a single licensed inn with a garden, piggeries and out-buildings situated near the wire works. (The wire works was situated where the Territorial Army Barracks is today) The inn was auctioned at the Halfway Hotel on Tuesday 26th March 1878. In September of the same year the license was transferred from Jesse Holder to William Bevan who, in July 1879 instructed auctioneers to sell all of his household possessions as he was leaving Cwmbran for America. Items for sale included – kitchen tables and chairs, dinner and tea services, cutlery, an eight day clock, a mahogany dining room suite, dining table, walnut drawing room suite, cottage pianoforte, clocks, ornaments, occasional tables, engravings, five iron French bedsteads, feather beds, mahogany and painted chests of drawers, wash stands, dressing tables, toilet glasses and many other effects.

Edmund Jones had moved into the Hollybush Inn by the time of the 1881 census with his wife, Sarah. He gave his occupation as a factory worker but by the time of the 1891 census he was listed as an innkeeper.

In October 1883 Edmund Jones was summoned for allowing drunken behaviour on his premises. The magistrates though, after hearing all the evidence, dismissed the case.

This next story from the South Wales Echo of 29 September 1888 does not really involve the Hollybush Inn until the very end. However it is an interesting insight into life in Cwmbran.

The story concerns William Evans, an old man, who was charged with shooting William Green. Green, a hawker, was out with his wife when he was stopped by Evans who offered to 'toss a coin for a pint of beer'. Green obliged but Evans lost.

About five hours later Green saw Evans near his house. Evans then asked Green if he was going to pay for the beer. Green refused as Evans had lost fair and square so Evans attacked him. Green then found a stone and threw it at Evans, hitting him in the head, to which Evans shouted – 'Where's my gun!'
Evans ran up the yard to his house to get it. He then ran after the Greens, taking aim. He fired and Mr Green felt he was shot in the back of his head. He fell to his knees but with his wife's help managed to get back up. Evans was eventually arrested by Police Sergeant Pask at the Hollybush Inn.

Edmund Jones kept the Hollybush Inn for a few more years. He and his wife were still there on the 1901 census. By the time of the 1911 census William Corsley was the landlord who lived there with his wife Rachel and children – Sydney and William.

There is no mention of 4 Two Locks Road on the 1939 Register, so presumably it had ceased to exist by then.

Rose and Crown

The Rose and Crown Hotel, Victoria Street, was probably built sometime in between 1861 and 1863. There is no mention of it on the 1861 census however it was recorded in local newspapers in July 1863 as one of the places the injured of the rail crash of that month were taken to.

It was next mentioned in the news in the 28th December issue of the Monmouthshire Merlin when three men – Jesse Sadler, David Harrison and Edward Harrison appeared in court charged with having assaulted a woman named Mary Parker. Landlord Charles Coles said that Mary and her husband had been drinking from five-thirty in the evening until eight-thirty. Eventually he refused to serve them any further as they were drunk.

Mary's husband then caused a row by hitting one of the three men and by drinking out of a pint vessel that did not belong to him. He also hit the landlord in the eye which prevented him from seeing for three days. The three men were discharged while Mary and her husband had to pay the court costs.

We can never know if this incident was the reason Charles Coles gave up the Rose and Crown but not long after it was taken over by Robert

Drink!

A Walk Around the Historic Inns of Cwmbran

Carol Ann Lewis

OTHER PUBLICATIONS

NON -FICTION

CWMBRAN – HISTORY AND MYSTERY
GWENT – HISTORY AND MYSTERY
VICTORIAN CWMBRAN
VICTORIAN PONTYPOOL
HAUNTING TALES
TELL THEM OF US
LAND OF MY MOTHERS
VICTORIAN DOMESTIC ABUSE
SURVIVOR AND OTHER POEMS
CHILDREN OF NATURE – A HISTORY OF WITCHCRAFT
CHRISTMAS PAST
CHRISTMAS IN MONMOUTHSHIRE

FICTION

HANBURY PARK
EDINA GREEN IN THE AFTERLIFE
KISSING FROGS

A long time ago, when Cwmbran was just a group of scattered villages and farms, it had thirty-eight public houses. Had you gone on a pub crawl and tried to have a pint in each, you probably would not have made it.

The public house was the hub of the community, it provided an income for families, refreshments for travellers and workers. It was a meeting place for clubs and associations. It was a place for people to meet, not just to drink but to talk, play sports, sing, dance, play music. hold competitions, fall in love, have wedding receptions. They were places that treated the injured, that took in lodgers, that held inquests on dead bodies.

With the building of Cwmbran New Town, many of these old original pubs were demolished and a lot of history was lost.

Today there are just thirteen left and even some of the new pubs that replaced them have been demolished or turned into housing.

This book takes you on a journey around them all.

Sawtell, aged thirty-eight from Poulton, Somerset. He was recorded on the 1871 census with his wife Catherine and four children – Charles, eight, Elizabeth, six, Benjamin, four and James who was five months old. They also employed a servant, Ann Rodell who was twenty-one.

In September 1872 an inquest was held by Mr Brewer, coroner, on an unknown man who had died on the tenth of the month. Daniel James Baker, police constable. said he had called at the Rose and Crown at 10.35 pm, staying until 10.52 pm when the landlord began to close up for the night. He saw the man in the kitchen who told him that he had asked Mr Sawtell for a pipe of tobacco half an hour earlier. The constable handed him some, the man put it in his pipe, lit it and walked out perfectly sober. The constable later passed him on the bridge over the train line (now the Cwmbran Drive) where he said nothing. The constable heard no more until the man was picked up off the train tracks at 6.40 the next morning. He was suffering from concussion and died later at Newport Hospital.

Many social gatherings were held at the hotel. In January 1873 the puddlers of the Patent Nut and Bolt works held their annual supper at the Rose and Crown where an 'excellent meal' was provided by Mr and Mrs Sawtell. The workmen were congratulated on their prosperity while those in other parts of the country could barely afford life's basics.

The census of 1881 records three more children for the Sawtells – Alfred, seven, Ada, five and Kate, three. There was also a servant, Eliza Lear, aged fifteen who was Robert Sawtell's niece.

The Rose and Crown was in the news again the following year. In May 1882, Thomas Stevens, a labourer was 'drunk and riotous' on the premises and refused to leave which led to a fine of ten shillings.

Then in 1883 it made the news twice. In May of that year Mr Brewer held an inquest at the police station regarding the death of William Edwards who had died at the station on 17th April. On the day, Edwards had gone to the Halfway Hotel where landlord, Mr Brooker had told him to go home as he was drunk. He didn't though, instead he went to the Rose and Crown where Mr Sawtell didn't notice his condition and served him some beer. Edwards did not drink it all but gave some to a friend. From the Rose and Crown he was carried to a railway fence and left there, later being moved to the police station. During the night he was visited a few times by Police Constable Lawrence who found his condition to be worsening. He sent for a doctor who requested that hot bricks should be placed on Edwards's feet but it was to no avail.

A post mortem was carried out on the 22nd and he was later buried. The doctor said at the inquest Edwards had died from blood on his brain.

Seven months later the Rose and Crown was burgled!

A quiet period followed as far as news stories go. In May 1894 the men of the fire brigade held their annual dinner at the hotel. So too did members of Cwmbran Football Club in 1896, in order to elect officers for the coming season.

On the 25th June 1900, Robert Sawtell died and Catherine became landlady. The license for the premises was transferred to her in August 1900. The 1901 census showed she had three of her children still living with her as well as a servant, Annie Payne.

Tragedy struck in 1907. Mrs Charlotte Davies of 64 Victoria Street was due to go away on a trip with her husband. He had left her to go to the train station to get tickets while she went to the Rose and Crown to leave their house keys with the landlady for safe keeping. When she did not arrive at the station to meet her husband he went to look for her. He found her in the yard of the hotel, she was dead. Dr. Murphy was called and certified her death. Strangely he thought her death not suspicious and therefore no inquest needed. He diagnosed her as having heart disease.

Catherine Sawtell was in her seventies when Mr J.W.Everett, solicitor of Pontypool applied for the transfer of the license to her son in law, George Waters who had married her daughter Ada. George Waters was head of the household on the 1911 census with Ada assisting in the family business. They had three children at this time – Robert,six, Dorothy Catherine,four and Lilian,two. They had a servant, Emily Toms and Catherine Sawtell also lived with them, aged seventy-four as she would do until her death on 7th April 1916.

The 1939 register shows Edith Harris as the landlady. She was a fifty-four year old widow

The Rose and Crown survived as a public house into the 2000's. The last time I can remember going in there was around 2009. At the time of writing it is closed but being used as a dwelling.

Oakfield Inn

The first mention in old newspapers of the Oakfield Inn was in the Illustrated Usk Observer of 10th October 1863 when the Shepherd on the Hill Lodge held their anniversary gathering there. Around a hundred and twenty people sat down to supper provided by the landlord and his wife, Mr and Mrs Williams. Mr T Leadbetter was the chairman for the night and proposed loyal and patriotic toasts while entertainment was provided by harpist William Thomas of Merthyr.

Like many pubs in the 19th century the Oakfield Inn was used as a place to conduct inquests into deaths. Such was the case in June 1866 when Samuel Whittington, a middle aged man employed by Hill and Batt was drowned in the canal by the Halfway Hotel. He was taken out of the water quite quickly and surgeon J.S. Cousins called for but by the time he arrived the man had died. A verdict of accidental drowning was returned.

By 1871 the Oakfield had passed to William Bevan, thirty-four. The census of that year showed him living there with his wife, Sarah, also thirty-four and children Mary, Samuel, Ann and Eliza. There was also a servant employed, Elizabeth Morgan aged sixteen. On the next census in 1881 the inn was being run by Benjamin Lewis, thirty-four and his wife Margaret, twenty-eight. On the first day of January 1886, the Pontypool Free Press reported great hardship among local people due to a depression in the local industries. A meeting had been held on Thursday 24th December for the purpose of taking steps to alleviate the distress being felt. Notes were issued to deserving applicants to obtain supplies from local traders. One of these traders was the Oakfield Inn where bread and soup could be received.

By 1883 the landlord of the Oakfield Inn, John Lyons, was also victim to the depression. His business had been doing well but with the closure of the wire works customers became fewer and he became insolvent. He left the Oakfield Inn to become caretaker at the Forge Hammer public house. As for his debt his wife's money was used to pay some of it but even after that he still owed three hundred and fifty-five pounds seven shillings and six pence. His assets came to eighty-seven pounds and thirteen shillings leaving a deficiency of two hundred and eighty pounds four shillings and five pence. In court he made no offer and the case was adjourned.

In 1887 Emma Clark was landlady. In May of that year she was summoned at Caerleon petty sessions for selling beer during prohibited hours. Witness P.C. Watkins said he saw a man leaving the house after 11 p.m. with a jar containing half a gallon of beer. The defence was that the beer was a gift for a friend who was going to America. Emma wasn't fined but had to pay the court costs.

The Oakfield had another landlady by 1891. She was Sarah Malmloff aged thirty-six. She was married to Lars Malmloff a mariner from Malmo, Sweden. The 1891 census shows they had three children – William, Lars and Francis. A servant was also employed, Elizabeth Jenkins aged nineteen.

Being a landlady was a tough job as can be ascertained from a report in the South Wales Echo in February 1891. Thomas Scott was charged at Caerleon police court with assaulting Sarah. He had been in her pub using 'strong language' and she had asked him to moderate it three times before she took him by the shoulders and threw him out. After this wound to his dignity he returned and tried to hit her but a customer intervened and took the blow. Thomas then rushed at her and grabbed her by the throat choking her until she was unconscious. It took five customers to get him to release his grip. He said to the court that she had scratched his face and poked her finger in his eye which irritated him. He admitted to seizing her by the collar of her dress. She however, did not wish to press charges and he was let off with a ten shilling fine.

John Bryant was landlord in 1891 also. In June that year he applied for a music and dancing license. Mr Baker-Jones on behalf of Llantarnam Urban District Council opposed the request as did Superintendent James for the police. However the bench granted a license for Saturdays and Mondays for instrumental music and dancing only.

The 1901 Kelly's Trade Directory named Thomas John Pritchard as landlord for this year, however the license for the Oakfield was transferred in late 1904 to Edmund Jones, former landlord of the Hollybush Inn.

Before his departure Thomas Pritchard found the Oakfield making the news again. Edward Williams, a wire drawer was summoned for being drunk at the inn on 23 March. However Williams had arrived there already drunk so no charges were brought against Pritchard Police Sergeant Morris said he had followed Williams to the Oakfield after he had been thrown out of another pub. He had three previous convictions for drunkenness and was fined ten shillings.

The Oakfield changed hands again by the time of the 1911 census. It revealed the building had eight rooms and was home to John Jones, thirty-two, his wife Alice, twenty-eight, and his sister in law Annie Perry, twenty.

The original village of Oakfield was situated on Llandowlais Street between Two Locks and the railway line, now the Cwmbran Drive. Rows of houses hugged the sprawling mass of the Oakfield Wire Works, later Whitehead, Hill and Co, the site of which is now occupied by the territorial army centre. As to the location of the Oakfield Inn, old ordnance survey maps show a public house in the vicinity of the Jade Garden takeaway.

Waterloo Inn

According to internet sources, the Waterloo was built in 1810. It was originally a farm called Waterloo House. Built close to the canal though, it served the boatmen with refreshments.

The first evidence there is of this is on the 1851 census. Edward Evans, forty-six, lived there with his wife, Mary and children – Charles, ten, Henry, nine, Ann, five and infant, Edward. Edward Evans's occupation was given as a farmer and publican.

By the time of the 1871 census, Waterloo House had passed to the Carver family of Buckland Somerset. Charles Carver was fifty-two, his wife, Sarah, fifty and their son Charles, twenty-two.

It is lost in the mists of time as to whether Charles Carver continued farming at the Waterloo. It seems from Victorian newspapers that it became solely a public house.

There is a story in the County Observer of 5th August 1876 where

William Thomas was charged with assaulting Charles Carver on the 25th July. Thomas went to the Waterloo at 11 p.m. and because Carver refused to give him beer, he assaulted him and knocked him down. He was sent to jail for fourteen days.

Charles Carver was assaulted again in 1880. This was reported in the Cardiff Times of 27th November. Carver stated a disturbance had occurred in his house due to a man, William Morgan, drinking another man's beer. When Carver intervened and ordered Morgan out he punched him on the side of his head. Morgan was fined two shillings plus costs.

Charles Carver was around seventy years of age when he was summoned to Caerleon petty sessions for selling beer during prohibited hours. The story was recorded in the South Wales Daily News of 9th April 1887. At 10.30 p.m. On the 26th March, P.C. Watkins watched a woman go into the Waterloo beer house and return with a pint of beer in a tin mug. P.C. Watkins stopped the woman and asked her who had served her the beer to which she replied 'the old man', meaning Mr Carver. He walked the woman back to the pub and questioned Mr Carver who said that if she had not been begging so much he would not have served her. He was fined twenty shillings.

Later in November 1887, Charles Carver was summoned again to Caerleon petty sessions for supplying beer to a man named Tudor Williams, who was already drunk. P.C. Watkins reported that he had visited the Waterloo and found Williams in a 'very drunken state'. He was in possession of half a pint of beer which he admitted was his.

Mr Watkins, solicitor, appeared for Charles Carver, called two witnesses who denied that Williams had been supplied with drink. The case was dismissed by magistrates who thought there was doubt surrounding the affair but Carver still had to pay court costs.

As for Tudor Williams, he was summoned for being drunk at the Waterloo and evidence from the former case was repeated. Williams did not appear, his mother attended court to answer to the chairman. She said her son had been before the magistrates before and probably would again. Williams was fined twenty shillings but as there was no money to pay his mother offered to take the punishment.

The last mention of Charles Carver was as a seventy-three year old on the 1891 census. By the time of the 1901 census Charles Valentine Carver had taken over the Waterloo. He was a widower aged fifty-two with three children – Agnes, twenty-six, Thomas, nineteen and William, fourteen. They also employed a servant, Elizabeth Jones, nineteen.

Charles Valentine Carver died on December 28th 1904. His will was proved by his daughter Emily the value being forty-seven pounds and two shillings.

The license of the Waterloo then passed to Agnes Carver who was still the landlady on the 1911 census. Aged thirty-six, she was single and lived with her brothers, Thomas and Samuel. The census also provided further information about the pub by recording the number of rooms, which was eight.

On the 1939 register the Waterloo was occupied by Theophilus J Leonard aged forty-seven and his wife Maud, aged forty-one.

At two hundred and ten years old the Waterloo is one of the oldest buildings in Cwmbran and is still going strong in serving the community.

Railway Inn

The Railway Inn was situated on Llandowlais Street near to the Waterloo and Oakfield Inns.

The earliest mention of it was on the 1871 census when Rachel Whittaker was landlady. She was a widow aged seventy from Mamhilad and lived with her son William aged forty. They also employed a servant, Susannah who was aged eighteen.

The annual licensing sessions for Caerleon took place on 24th August 1888 before Mr F. J. Mitchell of Llanfrechfa Grange. The area of Caerleon also included Cwmbran. The population as at the census of 1881 showed there was seven thousand six hundred and forty two inhabitants with fifty licensed premises to serve them. An objection was made to the renewing of the license of the Railway Inn as the holder had been proceeded against and had left the country.

The license was renewed however and by the beginning of 1889 Henry Townsend was the landlord. He lived with his wife, Mary and had quite a fiery relationship as can be seen from a report in the South Wales Echo of 7th February 1889.

At Caerleon police court, Mary, described as a 'young, married woman of respectable appearance' was summoned for being drunk and using obscene language. P.C. Wall stated that she had been arguing in the street with her husband. A servant was called who denied Mary was drunk as did Mary herself. The case was adjourned.

The Townsends made the news again in July 1889. Henry Townsend was summoned to Caerleon police court for allowing riotous behaviour on his premises. P.C. Wall said that on the 1st July, just after 10 p.m. He went to the inn and heard a great commotion. There were loud cries of 'murder!' and 'police!' and what the officer described as a general uproar. Inside he found Henry Townsend on the floor with his brother-in-law, Nolan, on top of him. He separated the pair and sent Nolan out.

In court Mr Lyndon Moore appeared for Nolan and explained that Nolan was in the habit of sleeping at the inn and came to the house that night, drunk. He had been to a fete in Llantarnam. He was refused more drink and so began the disturbance to which Nolan pleaded guilty.

On the same evening William Jones, Thomas Morgan and Michael Purcell were also summoned for refusing to leave the inn. They had also been to the fete which was in aid of Llantarnam church and held in the grounds of Llantarnam Abbey. Henry Townsend ordered them to leave through a back door which they did but then went around to the front door and entered the house again.

Meanwhile Mary Townsend was charged with being drunk and disorderly on the same evening. She had been to the fete as well and once back at the inn abused P.C. Wall and staggered around in a drunken state.

Two witnesses appeared for Mary and denied she was drunk. Her case was dismissed along with the cases against Henry, Thomas Morgan, William Jones and Michael Pursell. Nolan was fined 20 shillings plus costs.

Henry Townsend appeared at Caerleon police court again in January 1890. This time he was charged with assaulting Mary on December 15th 1889. Mary said that Henry had been drinking a lot. He attacked her, hitting her with his fist in the face giving her two black eyes. She told the court she was too afraid to live with him as he threatened to kill her. She asked for a judicial separation, The magistrates treated the case as aggravated assault and granted a separation order. Henry was fined forty shillings and was ordered to pay Mary ten shillings a week towards her maintenance.

By the end of 1890 the license of the Railway Inn had changed hands, this time to Ann Debrett who was mentioned in the Pontypool Free Press of 12th December 1890. At Caerleon police court Catherine Abbis was fined twenty shillings and costs for assaulting Ann on the 16th November 1890.

The 1891 census recorded a new landlord. George Hutchings was thirty-three and from Somerset. He had a wife, Hannah, twenty-three and children – Beatrice, three, William, one, and Ann, four months. By the next census in 1901 Hannah was the license holder which suggests her husband had died. Their daughter Beatrice was thirteen but William and Ann who would have been eleven and ten were not listed. There were four other children though – Kitty, six, Phyllis, four, Grove, two and Daisy, ten months. Hannah also had her parents living with her, William and Ann Debrett. There was also a servant – Elizabeth Brown, seventeen.

Hannah was assaulted in September 1903. James Smith, a collier was the one fined for doing so. She was represented in court by Mr Lyndon Moore who stated that James came into the inn and demanded a drink. Hannah asked him to leave but he refused. He caught hold of her by the throat and bit her finger. The bench said license holders must be protected from violent people so James was fined six pounds or two months in prison.

Hannah's father, William was landlord on the 1911 census. He was seventy years old and a widower. The inn was also now called the Railway Hotel. William lived with daughter Beatrice who had married George Jones. They had one daughter, May, aged two. Also listed was Phyllis Hutchings, grand-daughter, fourteen, Grove Hutchings, grandson, twelve, Daisy Hutchings, grand-daughter, ten and servant Mary Meredith, twenty-three. The census also stated the hotel had nine rooms.

On the 1939 register, William Strickland, fifty-five resided there with his wife May, thirty-five. It was eventually demolished with the building of the new town.

Morning Star Inn

This inn was situated at the end of Star Street, Old Cwmbran. It probably got its name from the opening of a new Oddfellows lodge in October 1859. The wire works was nearing completion and it was believed a new lodge would be beneficial for the growing workforce.

Called the Morning Star Lodge, its opening ceremony took place at the Abbey Hotel by Isaac Williams. Then, after business was discussed about eighty people, mostly agents of the works, sat down to supper. Mr Davis Prosser was elected chairman. Toasts were given and music provided by a harpist. Songs were sung in both English and Welsh.

The Morning Star inn first appeared on the 1891 census. It's landlord was Charles Sawtell, twenty-seven who was both a publican and a boilermaker. He lived with his wife Mary. There was also a Star Cottage.

In October 1892 the Llanyravon estate came up for sale with various properties and pieces of land being auctioned. A Mr Sawtell, presumably Charles, bought pasture near the inn for two hundred and five pounds.

Charles Sawtell gave up being a publican by the time of the 1901 census. He was shown as living at 10 Malpas Street. The landlord of the now 'Star' Inn was Stephen Baker aged thirty-five.

On the 1911 census the landlord was Charles Howells aged thirty-three. The premises was recorded as having five rooms.

There was no mention of a Star Inn on the 1939 register, however there were two Star cottages, both now demolished.

The Abbey Hotel

The Abbey Hotel was probably built in the late 1850's. The first mention of it in old newspapers was from the Monmouthshire Merlin regarding the opening of the Morning Star Lodge in 1859. Mr Isaac

Williams was the first landlord. At the time of the 1861 census he and his wife Sarah were both forty-five years old.

In the summer of 1863, the hotel played a part in the train crash, when a West Midlands train crashed into the station that once stood on the now Cwmbran Drive. The most seriously hurt passenger, Edward Foxall, a commercial traveller from the Forest of Dean had severe head injuries and was taken, unconscious, to the hotel.

A large group of workmen employed at Oakfield wire works gathered at the hotel in April 1864. The purpose was to present the manager, Thomas Leadbetter with a gift. He was well worthy of the honour bestowed on him according to the Monmouthshire Merlin. The gift was a gold watch to the value of twenty pounds and also a gold ring for his wife.

At the time of the 1881 census, Isaac Williams was still landlord. He and his wife were now sixty-five years old. Isaac's profession was given as an innkeeper and a farmer. Hie niece Elizabeth Evans was employed as a barmaid, she was thirty-six and a widow. She lived at the hotel with her daughter, Mary Ann aged eleven. A servant was also employed, Amy Lloyd aged twenty-six.

Later that year Isaac Williams was charged by Susan Stead with assaulting her. He was fined fifteen shillings and was further charged with being drunk on his premises and fined ten shillings.

The Abbey Hotel made the news again in November 1888. The South Wales Echo recorded that Henry Watkins, a carpenter was summoned for being drunk and disorderly. P.C. Morgan had found him lying on the road after being turfed out of the hotel. The judge concluded he must be a wealthy young man as he had been fined several times before. He was fined a further twenty shillings or fourteen days in prison.

The Abbey Hotel was put up for sale by public auction on Thursday 29th August 1889. It contained on the ground floor a large bar, a smoke room, a large tap room, kitchen, scullery and pantry. On the first floor there was a large club room, three bedrooms and a large sitting room. Outside were out-houses, stables and toilets. The whole property was set in an area of two hundred and sixty one square yards. The hotel was for sale due to its landlord James Wilkes Wilson of Tewkesbury being under notice to leave the premises. It was also described as being one of the best houses in the district, doing a large trade.

A further description of the land surrounding the Abbey Hotel was given in the South Wales Daily News of February 1890. Two pieces of pasture land between the hotel and the wire works were available to let.

By the 1891 census Thomas McGuire was the landlord. He was forty-nine and lived with his wife, Harriet, forty-six. They had two children – Dora, eight and Owen, seven. By October 1896 though Harriet was a widow and the landlady of the hotel, A report in the South Wales Daily

News of the time tells of how she was sued at Newport County Court. Joseph Wallace, a brick layer tried to sue her for fifty pounds damages from a dog bite. Joseph said he had been passing the Abbey Hotel one evening in June when the dog, a large mongrel, jumped out and seized the thumb of his left hand. He said he had to hit the dog on the head before it would let go. His thumb was fractured in two places. He was a contractor in the brick works and as well as wages received a profit on work done by other men. As a result of the injury the works were closed for a month. To defend Mrs McGuire several witnesses appeared who said Joseph was drunk and had set his own dog on the landlady's dog and he had been bitten while interfering in the fight. The judge however said that Joseph had told a consistent story and gave judgement in his favour of eighteen pounds plus costs.

Harriet McGuire was still landlady into the 20th century with Dora working there as a waitress. At the age of fifty-eight she was still dealing with unruly customers such as Frank Coleman, a collier who was fined twenty shillings or fourteen days for disorderly conduct and refusing to leave when requested. Harriet stated that he had called her 'bad names' and when asked to clear out refused to do so.

This could be the reason why in January 1904 at the transfer of licenses sessions in Caerleon, Harriet, described in the Evening Express as an 'elderly woman who had held the license for fifteen years' asked to transfer it to her son. Thomas King McGuire. He had run public houses in Stourpoint, Worcestershire with police satisfaction and so the license as transferred to him.

The Abbey changed hands again by the time of the 1911 census this time to Walter Fryers. He was forty-seven and lived with his wife Florence, twenty-six and their two children, Leslie, three and John, two. The census also recorded that the hotel had seven rooms. The Fryers also employed two servants, Lily Bishop, nineteen and Lily Cooper, twenty-three.

When the First World War broke out in 1914 Walter was called up to fight. It then appeared the family may have fallen into financial difficulties as in January 1916 a company called James Straker and Son were selling by auction for Lieutenant Fryers a large part of his furniture and outdoor possessions. The Abergavenny Chronicle listed what was being auctioned, it included – a donkey, Governess car, an antique brass mounted dresser, a Chippendale mahogany bookcase bureau, dining room suite, upright pianoforte, a fireproof safe and other lots which included contents of the kitchen and reception rooms, two satin bedroom suites and bedsteads.

The Abbey Hotel had William T R Powell aged thirty-six as landlord on the 1939 register. He lived with wife Christina. The hotel was also well known for its Monkey Puzzle tree however this was destroyed when the hotel was demolished during the construction of the Cwmbran Drive.

The Mount Pleasant Inn

The first mention of houses with the name Mount Pleasant was on the 1851 census when there were two. The first dwelling was home to David Jones, a forty-two year old boatman and his wife Elizabeth, forty-one. In the second house lived David Llewellyn, an eighty-four year old tailor, his wife, Rachel, fifty-six and sons James, twenty-nine and William, twenty-five.

There was a slight change on the 1861 census. Number one Mount Pleasant still belonged to David Jones, he was no longer a boatman though but a proprietor of houses. Number two Mount Pleasant was occupied by William Howells, a twenty-seven year old roll turner and his wife Maria, twenty-five.

The two houses became one by the 1871 census and from this point became known as the Mount Pleasant Inn. The landlord at this time was James King, thirty-two and his wife, Emma.

In September of 1878 James took legal action against Francis Service of the Halfway Hotel and Walter Walters, a grocer. Both had applied for licenses to sell beer to be consumed off the premises. Both applications were opposed by Mr A J David acting on behalf of James and both applications refused.

James King died before the 1881 census. His wife Emma became landlady. Helping with the running of the inn was her mother in law, Sarah, aged seventy-three and servant, Martha Matthews aged sixteen.

Drunkenness was common and a couple of cases were reported in the papers for the inn. The first was recorded in the South Wales Daily News of October 1883 and concerned William Slade who was fined ten shillings and the next was William Monk in March 1884 who was fined twenty shillings.

On the 1891 census the inn changed hands and was occupied by the quite large Howells family. James Howell was the head aged forty-seven. He lived with wife Delia, forty-two and children Charles, thirteen, Amelia, eleven, Catherine, nine, Ada, seven, William, three, Maud, two and Albert, two months. There were also step-daughters Emily Davies, twenty who worked as the barmaid and Mariah Davies, twenty-seven plus servant Catherine Miskell aged twenty.

The Howells were considered a very kind family, well involved with the community. The Pontypool Free Press recorded one of their acts of kindness in May 1892 when they loaned their piano to Elim Congregational church for evening entertainment after their annual tea meeting.

In August 1895 the Mount Pleasant was at the centre of a court case involving a stabbing. At Caerleon police court five magistrates investigated a charge against Thomas Protheroe, a roller-man, Sarah Thomas, his sister and Catherine White, his niece. They were charged with wounding a man named Prosser Jones.

Jones appeared unwell during the trial and said on the evening of 27th July he went to Protheroe's house in Stone Row to ask why he had not spoken to him that day. At the house, he was hit from behind causing him to fall down in a senseless state. When he regained consciousness, Protheroe was by his legs and the two women by his shoulders. He felt a knife cutting into his thigh. Altogether he was stabbed seven times. Jones admitted he had been drinking a lot that day. Besides stab wounds he had injuries to the back of his head. Witness George Williams, who had been drinking in the Mount Pleasant said that Protheroe had borrowed a knife from him in the pub and as he left said, 'I have borrowed this knife from this man and you will hear more about it'. Witness Daniel Stevens saw Jones and Protheroe in the inn but ignored them. Protheroe gave the appearance of being sober but Daniel had seen him in the Mount three times that day.

Protheroe was committed for trial at the assizes in the Shire Hall, Monmouth in November 1895 where he pleaded guilty to unlawful wounding.

When the census was taken in 1901 Delia Howells was a widow and landlady of the Mount. She lived with her son Tom, twenty-five, daughter Rose, fifteen, William, thirteen and Maud, eleven.

The Mount underwent improvements and alterations in the following years. It was mentioned at the annual licensing meeting in Caerleon before magistrates J. Mitchell and F.M. Pilliner. These improvements may have been enforced by the court as progress was being monitored with reports from the police.

Delia Howells was still landlady on the 1911 census. Extra information recorded she had been married twice and had given birth to twelve children. Only one of those children remained with her at the inn and that was Maud who worked as a servant. The census also showed that the Mount had eight rooms.

The licensee on the 1939 register was Amelia Williams who was sixty years old. There was also John Williams, twenty-eight, a painter and decorator.

The Mount Pleasant, situated on Wesley Street is a quiet pub and still open today.

Halfway Hotel

The Halfway Hotel was probably built around the 1840's. Situated at the half way point along the Monmouthshire and Brecon canal it served the thirsty boatmen transporting coal and iron along the waterway.

The first mention of it in the Monmouthshire Merlin was on the 2nd September 1848. On a Wednesday night that month a foot race of fifty yards took place at the 'Halfway House' between Henry Williams and John Collier who was also known as the 'Monmouthshire Stag', for five pounds a side. A large number of people gathered to watch the race and the 'Stag' was the winner by a yard and a half.

It was mentioned again in the Monmouthshire Merlin of 28th October 1848. A letter was sent to the editor of the paper by 'E.R', wanting to know what was done with the fines given to several people for riots at the Halfway House and at Springvale. The fines amounted to eighteen pounds.

The next mention in the Monmouthshire Merlin was on 4th November 1848 where it was referred to as the Halfway Inn rather than 'House'. A party of gentlemen connected with Cwmbran Ironworks met at the 'house of Mr H Williams' to celebrate according to custom the night of 'Nas cyn-y-gayaf'. This was probably Noson Galan Gaeaf the Welsh 'Winter's Eve', celebrating the end of Autumn and beginning of Winter or Halloween as we would know it today, A lavish supper was prepared and toasts were given by the Chairman for prosperity to the Cwmbran Works. Songs were sung and music was provided by musicians Messrs Silverthorne on the violin and flute. After a pleasant evening all retired to their homes.

On New Year's Day 1849 the very first meeting of Cwmbran Cymreigyddion took place. It was an eisteddfod held at the inn where a large crowd of people gathered along with bards from all parts of Wales. The meeting was scheduled for four o'clock but large groups accumulated well before then. Shortly after four the rooms were filled with around three hundred people.

First prize for the best ode went to Reginald Blewitt of Llantarnam Abbey who was also proprietor of Cwmbran Ironworks. Second prize went to Mr John Rees of Merthyr for his history of Llantarnam Abbey. Mr John Jones, forge manager of Cwmbran Ironworks took third prize for the best song. After prizes were awarded the rest of the evening was spent dancing to tunes played on the harp.

Later in the year, in October, the Ancient Order of Foresters Friendly Society sat down to an 'excellent dinner' provided by Mr and Mrs Williams. Toasts were given to both the queen and to success in the iron trade.

When the census was taken in 1851 the Halfway had a new landlord by the name of Charles Howells, aged fifty-three, He lived there with his wife, Ann, fifty and children – Charles, twenty-one, a butcher, Catherine,fourteen, Hannah, thirteen, Mary Ann, eleven, Elizabeth, nine and Thomas, seven. They also employed a servant, Elizabeth Thomas who was twenty-three.

Another gathering was recorded in the Monmouthshire Merlin for the inn in February 1860 and concerned the return of Mr Woodcock and his bride to their residence. They were welcomed by the firing of cannons and a firework display. A supper was held on the 13th ordered by Mr Woodcock for all his workmen and some of his neighbours which was provided by the Howells. The chairman gave a toast to Mr and Mrs Woodcock, the party then continued for several hours.

The Howells still occupied the Halfway on the 1861 census, though the family was smaller consisting of Charles, sixty-five, Ann, sixty-one, David, twenty-six, Hannah, twenty-three, Mary, twenty and Thomas, seventeen.

In July 1863 a terrific train crash occurred near to the Halfway. The track followed the route of what is now the Cwmbran Drive and a train station existed on the left hand side near the Rose and Crown. On that day a train had been travelling from Liverpool, passing through Pontypool where it picked up more passengers. As it approached Cwmbran, eye witnesses described it as appearing to come off the rails as it went under the Halfway Bridge and mounted the station platform, smashing carriages against each other. The driver, Robert McGhee was killed instantly. Many of the victims were taken to the Halfway while the inquest held in order to formally identify the body of McGhee was held there too.

The inn appears to be unoccupied on the 1871 census but was open in 1878 as inquests were being held there. Two took place in April 1878 conducted by coroner, Mr Brewer. The first concerned Henry Davies, blacksmith, aged sixty-eight who had dropped down dead on a Sunday night. A little boy called Samuel Gillam stated he saw the deceased on the road and watched as he turned into a lane. He then fell down on his face. Samuel ran to him and tried to turn him over. On seeing the man was dead he became frightened and called out to another man called Day who took the body to his son's house. The jury returned a verdict of death by natural causes.

The second was held regarding the suspicious death of a baby boy, son of Widow Margaret Sullivan. He was born on the 2nd and buried as a stillborn child. On exhuming his body though, a post mortem found the baby had died from suffocation. Nanny Minahan of Oakfield gave evidence to say that the baby was born alive and well. Police Constable Seys reported that on the 4th he went to visit Margaret and was told the baby was buried at Pontnewydd churchyard. She also told him a man named Alfred Martin, who lived in the same house, took the body and buried it. The jury gave a verdict of death by suffocation but there was no evidence to show how.

The landlord in 1879 was James Brooker. He was taken to court in March of that year by Mr Kerry, a wine and spirit merchant from Bristol. The claim was for seven pounds, the value of a quarter cask of whisky. It was stated that in November 1874 an agent of Mr Kerry called at he Halfway and received an order for the whisky in question. However Brooker refused to pay and the cost remained 'in bond'. Brooker said that the agent pressed him very much to purchase it but he refused. He later received an invoice and he believed, returned it. When being cross examined Brooker denied promising to send the agent a cheque. He revealed he did not even have a bank account. Judgement was given for Brooker.

A tragedy occurred in April 1879. Between 9 and 10 o clock at night a man fell into the canal between Pontnewydd and Cwmbran and drowned. The body was taken to the Halfway and was later identified as a man from Blackwood, aged about 45 and a plasterer.

The 1881 census gave more information about James Brooker and family. He was thirty-eight at the time of the enumeration and was born in Middlesex. His wife was Charlotte, thirty-four from Gloucester. They had six children – Henry,eleven, Mary, nine, Anna, seven, Charles, five, George,three and Emma, one.

Mr Brewer held another inquest at the Halfway in August 1883. It concerned the death of Joseph Lucas who had been fighting with a man named Jeremiah Murphy. Witness, William Williams stated that on Saturday night he saw them fighting on the Halfway bridge. Lucas struck Murphy in the face twice. They were separated by P.C. Seys but while he was persuading Murphy to go home, Lucas hit him over the policeman's shoulder, knocking his helmet off. While P.C. Seys was retrieving his helmet the fight continued. Both men fell but Lucas complained he could not get up. He was taken home and attended to by Dr. Lloyd who stated the cause of death was dislocation of the spine. The jury returned a verdict of accidental death.

In January the following year the body of an elderly man was retrieved from the canal. He was about 60 years of age, five feet nine, grey hair and had whiskers. He was dressed in a black coat and trousers, cord vest, a check shirt and dark plaid scarf. His body was taken to the Halfway and lay there awaiting identification and an inquest.

In 1904 the Halfway had a manageress. She was mentioned in the Evening Express in March when it was decided by the licensing justices that the person responsible for managing the hotel should reside on the premises at night. The manageress was Miss Charlotte Edwards and the license was transferred to her. At the meeting Superintendent Jones said that he usually objected to women holding licenses but he was without objection in this case as Miss Edwards had kept the house very well for eight years.

On the 1911 the head of the household was John Wait, a sixty-one year old haulage contractor. His wife Charlotte, fifty-three, was manageress.

They employed a barmaid, Winifred Howell, twenty-three and two servants – Audrey Davies and Lillian Howard, both sixteen.

Harold James was listed on the 1939 register as living at the Halfway. He was a thirty-seven year old mental nurse who lived with wife, Mary, thirty-nine and son Kenneth, five. Also registered there was William Ellison, forty-three, manager of the biscuit works plus two servants – Gertrude Edwards, forty-four and Betty Challenger, twenty. The Halfway Hotel remains open to this day.

Mill Tavern

At the lower end of Coed Eva, on Mill Road once stood a mill complex known as Mill Farm. It consisted of the Mill Tavern or Mill Inn as it was known on early ordnance survey maps and a corn mill. Close by a large pond provided water to turn the wheels of the corn mill. It is possible the corn mill belonged to the monks of Llantarnam Abbey and could be as old as the 16th century. The Mill Inn though may have been a later addition. A tram road was built in 1818 to transport coal from Henllys colliery down along Two Locks Road to the brickworks and canal and the Mill Inn may have provided refreshments.

The 1851 census showed it was a farm of 21 acres. The head of the house was a fifty year old widow called Elizabeth Evans whose occupation was a farmer. She lived with her children - Edward, aged twenty-three and a rail inspector, Ann, twenty-one, John, the miller and George, fifteen. Mill Farm continued to be occupied by Elizabeth and her family for another twenty years at least.

It was not until the 1880's that the Mill Tavern was referred to as a licensed establishment in old newspapers. The earliest mention was in the County Observer of 30th September 1882 where magistrates granted the temporary transfer of the inn's license from G. Waters to Margaret Lewis.

We get a glimpse of the character of the Mill Tavern in the Western Mail of 28th August 1885. At the Caerleon licensing sessions, Captain Gurney, superintendent of police stated that all pubs in the area were well kept, except the Mill Tavern. Mr Watkins, a solicitor from Pontypool had applied for the renewal of the license but it was objected to by the police. Magistrates adjourned their decision for a month with the hope that a new tenant would take possession.

Two months later Mr Watkins appeared again to support the application for the renewal of the license. Superintendent Gurney opposed it on the grounds that the house was of a disorderly character. Also the present owner, John Gillard had been convicted the previous April when he was fined fifty shillings plus costs. Gillard said that he would leave the house by Thursday. Magistrates granted a license on condition it was transferred to a new tenant.

At the time of the 1891 census the inn had changed hands to Morgan Williams, aged thirty-three and a farmer. He lived with his wife Esther and their son Charles aged five.

In July 1892 three men – Patrick and John Desmond and Patrick McMullen were summoned for falsely representing themselves as travellers. The defendants, with five other men were thirsty on a Sunday afternoon and with public houses being closed there was nothing alcoholic available (unless you were 'travelling'). So they went to the Mill Tavern and said they were 'travellers'. They told the landlady they were from Abersychan and were going to Newport. They asked for some beer and gave false names. It was later revealed the men were from Cwmbran. McMullen was fined ten shillings. The Desmonds didn't appear before magistrates so were fined an extra five shillings.

The license of the Mill Tavern was transferred again in December 1896 to Mrs Mary Ann Davies. The bench commented on the fact that the license had been transferred half a dozen times in the previous two years and hoped she was aware of the fact.

The next known landlady was Sarah Hunt. In February 1900 she was charged with selling rum during prohibited hours on Christmas Day. P.C.Bowen said that at 5.35 p.m. he saw a girl named Alice Taylor go to the Mill Tavern and receive something from the defendant who he accused of selling half a pint of rum. Alice said the rum was wanted for someone who was unwell. The bench took a lenient view, there was no conviction and the defendant paid the costs.

In November 1900 William Davies made an application to Caerleon petty sessions for the transfer of the license from Sarah Hunt to himself which was granted.

By the 1901 census there was yet another licensee, Mary Thomas. She was forty-nine and lived with her children – Mary twenty-six, Albert, twenty-three, Elizabeth, twenty-three, Emily, fourteen, Sydney, thirteen and William, nine. Elizabeth also worked as the barmaid. Mary ran the Mill Tavern until March 1903 when she applied for a transfer of the license from herself to John Davies. She told the court the house was tied to Hancock's Brewery. She produced an agreement but it did not have the seal of Hancock's fixed to it. The magistrate's clerk said the document was 'useless' and only granted a temporary transfer. Eventually though the license went to John Davies permanently.

John Davies, forty-two and his wife, Jane, forty-nine, ran the Mill Tavern on the 1911 census. It also recorded that the inn had six rooms plus a cellar.

On the 1939 register William Cooper, sixty was the landlord living with wife, Mary, sixty-one and children William, thirty-eight and Margaret, thirty three.

The Mill Tavern closed in the late summer of 2011. It was demolished in November 2012 to make way for new housing.

Tennis Court Hotel

In the County Observer of the 7th March it was reported that an application had been made at the licensing sessions by Mr T Francis of the Old Green Hotel, Newport for a license for the premises to be known as the Tennis Court Hotel. It was situated on the main road between Llantarnam and Cwmbran. The application was opposed by Mr Corner on behalf of Mr Sawtell of the Rose and Crown, Mr McGuire of the Abbey Hotel, Mr G Llewellyn on behalf of Mr Humphreys of the Halfway Hotel and Mr H S Lyne on behalf of the police. The property was leased to Mr Francis by Cwmbran Building Society and if the license had been granted it was on condition the Abbey Hotel had to close. The application was refused.

In March 1904 the justices refused to grant a license again. This time the application was made by Mrs Fanny Jones, a Cardiff licensee. It was objected to by the police. It was also the fifth year in succession a license was refused.

January 1906, another application was made for the hotel, owned by Phillips and Sons brewers, Newport. The applicant was Mr Harris Bryant Bence, a butcher of Cardiff. Mr Lyne opposed on behalf of the police, Mr Hornby on behalf of Mrs McGuire, Abbey Hotel and Mr Evans of Newport represented residents in the vicinity of the proposed hotel. Also objecting were representatives of the Temperance party.

It was stated that since 1899 an application had been made every year for a license except 1902 and 1905 when Messrs Phillips bought the premises. Over time the building had become in a more important position owing to a road being built from Cwmbran to Pontnewydd. A number of engineers had come to the district repairing machines for the work etc, but there was nowhere for them to stay. The new hotel would save them having to go to Newport. The district had grown and had about seven thousand inhabitants. No new licences had been given for thirteen years. The hotel was also convenient for justices when they came to Cwmbran for court.

Mr John Martin Pritchard stated that he had built the hotel at a cost of five thousand pounds. His attempts to acquire a license failed and so he sold it in 1903 to Cwmbran Building Society but they sold it to Phillips. A first class hotel with billiard room was required in the district. Mr John Williams, an accountant at the brick works said the hotel would be a real convenience but the chairman disagreed and the application was refused again.

It does not appear that any more applications were made, so what became of the Tennis Court Hotel? It was not mentioned on the 1901 census, however there was recorded a 'new hotel, new shops and new houses close to Ventnor Road, Tilney Villa and Grange Road. The only clues available from the 1911 census are four houses that possibly refer to the builder – John Martin Pritchard and they were numbers 68, 70, 80 and 86 Llantarnam Road recorded on the 1911 census as 'Pritchard's Terrace'.

FORGEHAMMER

The Forgehammer Hotel

The Forgehammer Hotel was built around the mid 1800's. It was listed on the 1851 census and run by Benjamin Lewis, thirty-nine and his wife Jane, thirty-seven. They had two children – Benjamin, seven and Elizabeth, five. Benjamin's mother-in-law also lived with them. She was seventy-two and employed as a cook.

June 1854 was the anniversary of the Philanthropic Brethren. The day was windy with heavy rain but many attended Elim chapel and visited Llantarnam and Croesyceiliog. They then returned to the Forgehammer where dinner was provided by Benjamin Lewis. There was also music by a Newport band.

An inquest was held at the hotel in January 1856 by coroner W.H. Brewer. It concerned the Cwmbran forge manager, W. R. Davies. Some workmen had been fitting machinery in the loft of the lathing room. They were removing a block weighing about seventy pounds, one man handing it down to another, when one of the men did not get a proper grip on it and it fell to the ground floor through a trap door directly over the entrance through which Mr Davies was passing. The block hit him on the forehead fracturing his skull. He was badly injured and treated by surgeon, Mr Cousins. He did not recover though and died four days later.

Around this time, due to famine and poverty, many Irish families left their homeland and settled in places like Forgehammer, finding employment in the ironworks. In order to attend Mass they had to walk to Pontypool or Newport as there was no service in Cwmbran but in the 1860's a priest was approached to see if he would travel to Cwmbran every Sunday. To begin with Mass was said in a room in a bakery on Spring Street but later moved to a club room at the Forgehammer Hotel. This room was reached by a ladder, the ceiling was very low so heads often touched it. The floor was also rickety and before any Mass was said it had to be cleaned up from the many Saturday night club meetings first. Underneath the room was a stable where pigs were kept. This room was used for two years until the priest decided it would be a good idea to build a chapel.

Another inquest was held in October 1870 by Mr. Brewer on the body of John Power, an Irish labourer of Nightingale Row. He and another man, John O'Brien were staggering home drunk along the canal when both fell in. Their cries brought people to help and water was let out of the canal by the locks but John Power had drowned.

The next recording of the hotel was on the 1871 census. William Jones, thirty-one was the landlord. He lived with his wife Elizabeth, twenty-six, and children – Mary Ann, six, John, four and Benjamin, one

In May 1871 an inquest was held into the death of Thomas Thomas who died at the forge. Thomas was previously in business with his sister in Cardiff but left home to work in Cwmbran Forge. He had been working night shift and was engaged in wheeling cross ends of bars. The cross ends caught in the cog wheel of the engine working some shears. The barrow tipped up and he was thrown with it. He fell into the cog wheels, was carried around the cage and was crushed to death. He was buried at Cwmbran church.

In September 1875 a widows and orphans fund fete of the Lodge of Perseverance, Ancient Order of Shepherds was held in a field belonging to Mr Jones, near the station in Pontnewydd. Entries for the rustic sports were very few and not as anticipated.

William and Elizabeth Jones still lived at the hotel on the 1881 census. Their son Benjamin was listed as well as children born since the previous census – William, nine, Martha, seven, Elizabeth, five, Amy, three and Margaret, one. They also employed a servant, Elizabeth Attwell, nineteen.

A drowning occurred near the hotel in October 1899. Some young men were returning to Cwmbran from Pontnewydd about 9.30 pm when a splash was heard in the canal. As their friend Rosser was unaccounted for they raised the alarm. The man was found between the lock gate and the bridge leading to the Nut and Bold works. Once his body was retrieved it was apparent that he had hit his head. He was twenty-three and had recently opened a grocers shop.

It was all change on the 1901 census. James Gittings, thirty-eight was the landlord. With him was his wife Sara, thirty-six, and children – John, eight, Caroline, six, William, four, Lucy, three, and Winifred, one. Also listed was James's nephew William, a gardener aged thirty-six and Rosina Butcher, eighteen and a servant.

In September 1903 a concert was held at the hotel in connection with 'C' company of the 3rd Battalion, South Wales Borderers. Colour Sergeant Poole was presented with a silver mounted walking stick on the occasion of him leaving the battalion after twenty-one years of service.

Another presentation evening was held in August 1907. Captain A Sale presented Sergeant Pauncefort Mundy, who was leaving the South Wales Borderers, with an oak bookcase.

James Gittings continued to run the hotel on the 1911 census. The census also recorded the number of rooms which was fifteen. The hotel was still open during the time of the 1939 register and was run by Elias Newton, fifty-seven and wife Edith, fifty-nine. In the 1950's the landlord was John McGuire. The hotel survived until around the early 1970's when re-development of Forgehammer took place.

The Moon Inn

The Moon Inn was situated between the canal and the railway sidings in Forgehammer. The first mention in records was from the Illustrated Usk Observer of 19 May 1866. Landlord James Prosser was charged with having his house open during prohibited hours on the 4th. P.C. Howes proved the charge and Prosser was fined thirty shillings.

The landlord in 1870 was Timothy Leo. It was reported in the Monmouthshire Merlin of 4th November that a watch belonging to him had been stolen by William Davies. He was drinking at the inn when Leo handed his watch to him to see what time it was. Davies then put it into his own pocket and took it home. Leo didn't discover his watch was missing until he went to bed. He then went with a policeman to Davies's lodgings. Davies was sleeping in one room with five other men. He gave the watch back straight away. He was discharged with a caution as he said it had been a practical joke.

Timothy Leo was still landlord on the 1871 census. He was forty-one years old at the time and lived with his wife Hannah, thirty. They had two lodgers, George Lloyd, forty and Thomas Jones, fifty-five.

By 1879 John Lyons had taken over the hotel. In March that year he was charged with opening his house after hours. On the census in 1881 John Lyons was 34 years old and lived with his wife, Sarah, thirty-seven. They had four children – Rachel, thirteen, Thomas, eleven, Mary, nine and John, four.

In October 1882 George Doyle, John Murphy and John Driscoll were summoned for being drunk and disorderly. They were being riotous in the Moon and after being removed by P.C. Seys continued to fight in the street. Driscoll was fined five shillings and the other two, ten shillings.

John Butcher was landlord by 1884 but found himself in trouble for an infringement of the licensing law by permitting drunkenness at the inn but was dismissed with a caution. In October of the same year the license was transferred from him to Thomas Prosser.

Thomas Uniac, a labourer at the Patent Nut and Bolt works was charged with wounding David Cunningham on March 10th 1888. David said he was with his brother at the Moon Inn when a row started with Uniac over a puppy. They agreed to go out and fight and about five minutes later Uniac rushed at David with a knife which penetrated his waistcoat. He pushed Uniac away but he attacked him again and threw him down on his back. David rolled over on his and Uniac stabbed him five times. David called to his brother then fainted from blood loss.

Dr. Edmunds stated that David had three or four wounds to his buttocks and thighs. P.C. Wall who arrested Uniac found a blood stained knife at his home between his bed and mattress. In court Uniac was found guilty and sentenced to six weeks imprisonment.

On the 1891 census the landlord was George Moseley aged sixty. He lived with his wife Elizabeth, fifty-nine. They employed a servant, seventeen year old Jessie Sharp. By the end of the year though they had left and Thomas Williams had taken over. He was charged in December 1891 for supplying drink to a drunken man named John Williams. John was a relative and had lived at the inn for a few years. On the evening in question he had been out on business and returned home, no drink was given to him and the case was dismissed.

At Caerleon police court in March 1893 the landlord of the Moon applied to have the license transferred to Mrs Martha Williams. It was opposed however by Superintendent Bosanquet on the grounds that it was the roughest house in Cwmbran and a woman was not the proper person to manage it.

At Newport County Court in July 1893, Thomas Williams was charged with receiving barrels of beer from Williams Brothers and Buckley Brothers breweries and not paying for them. Williams stated business had been bad and he had only been able to sell one barrel a week. Williams owed twenty-one pounds and was made to pay in monthly installments of five pounds.

The following month a question of license at Caerleon police court. Mr Kinsey-Morgan, solicitor, applied for the license of the Moon Inn to be given to Frederick Pugh, however, Mr Webb, a solicitor representing Mr Hollyfield, a blind man, said Mr Hollyfield had paid twenty pounds in an agreement with Thomas Williams but he has been unable to get his money back. The case was adjourned but eventually the license went to Frederick Pugh.

Fred Pugh kept the Moon Inn until July 1894 when an application for the transfer of the license was granted to Daniel Plaisted.

When Daniel took over the Moon Inn he was new to the business. He was originally a moulder but had lost his leg in a railway accident the previous June. In September 1894, Zachariah Thomas staggered into the inn but he was ordered out. Zachariah's father asked Daniel if he could stay a couple of minutes while he finished his beer then he would take his son home. Daniel agreed but unfortunately the police arrived and so at Caerleon both Daniel and Zachariah appeared in court. Mr. Webb put in a strong plea for Daniel and the charges against him, supplying drink to a drunken man, were dropped upon payment of costs.

Daniel and family were still at the Moon Inn on the 1901 census. He was aged thirty-five and his wife Emily was thirty-three. Their children were – John, ten, Mary, eight, Elsie, three and Emily, six months. Also living with them was a cousin, Rose Burton, a twenty-two year old widow.

William and John Ryan, brothers, along with Llewellyn Hughes were summoned for being disorderly and refusing to leave the Moon Inn in March 1904. They were charged with assaulting the landlord and damaging windows to the value of twenty shillings. William Ryan was not present at court but a warrant was issued for his arrest. John was fined two pounds plus costs and Hughes one pound plus costs.

The Plaisted family were still at the Moon Inn on the 1911 census. They had two more children – Lucy, eight and Albert, three. The census also showed the Moon Inn had ten rooms. It was not listed on the 1939 register but that does not mean the building was not there it may have been a dwelling. Ultimately though it was demolished.

The Moulders Arms

Newspaper reports suggest the Moulder's Arms was built in the 1850's. An advertisement from 3rd April 1858 reads – 'To let next May, public house, near to the forge'.

The 1861 census gives more information as to its whereabouts in Cwmbran. On the enumerator's route it was situated between the Ebbw Vale Company House and Hopkins House near Forgehammer.

In early December 1865 it was the scene of a horrific crime. It was on a Sunday morning when rumours of a cold-blooded murder began to circulate. The previous night between nine and ten o clock, William Davies, aged twenty-seven, while drunk, was stabbed through the heart dying almost instantly. The perpetrator was nineteen year old Herbert Harper.

Evidence from witnesses was gathered but a lot was contradictory. Davies was said to have encountered a group walking towards him. He staggered drunk against some women which caused harsh words from the men of the group. A fight then ensued. Two women in the group also had words with Harper. He carried a knife and said he used it in self defence accidentally stabbing Davies.

An inquest was held at the Forgehammer Hotel. Witnesses stated they saw an injured Davies stagger into the Moulder's Arms. A woman, Mary Morgan, followed him and found him lying on a settle in the kitchen with his head down. She sat by him, lifted his head onto her knee where he died a few minutes later.

Witness, George Davies, a puddler at Cwmbran Forge was in the Moulder's Arms with William Davies. He said they heard fighting outside and ran to see what was going on. There, William had a scuffle with Harper. Another woman, Sarah Matthews caught hold of William and as Harper raised a knife at her, she stepped back but it cut the front of her dress. He then stabbed William.

After two hours the jury's verdict was manslaughter against Harper.

On 6th June 1868 the Moulder's Arms came up for auction. In the Monmouthshire Merlin it was no longer described as a public house but as a dwelling house with a good garden. The yearly rent was twenty pounds. It was described as being near to the ironworks adjoining Greenmeadow farm and a short distance from Pontnewydd railway station.

New Bridgend Inn

Situated by he canal in Forgehammer the New Bridgend or 'Bottom Bridge' was opened in 1849.

Rachel Davies was the landlady in 1870. In October of that year she was charged by Superintendent McIntosh for permitting drunkenness. John O'Brien stated he left work on 4th October at six in the evening and went to the inn with John Power. They were both drunk when they left at nine. They had had seven quarts of beer between them. As they crossed he canal they both fell in. John O'Brien was dragged to safety but John Power died. Rachel was fined forty shillings.

Rachel Davies was sixty-eight years old on the 1871 census. A widow, she lived with her son-in-law, Jesse Sadler, twenty-six, daughter Margaret, twenty-six and grandchildren – Evan,four, Ellen, two and Gertrude, nine months.

On August 28th 1875, John Desmond, a relative of the 'well known Dan Desmond' was committed for fourteen days for refusing to leave the Bridgend.

Rachel Davies was still landlady on the 1881 census. She was seventy-nine years old and lived with her grand daughters Rachel Lyons, thirteen, who worked as a servant, Ellen,twelve and Gertrude, eleven.

Rachel Davies died soon after the census and in the Monmouthshire Merlin of 6th October 1882 the inn was advertised for sale. It was described as an eight roomed beer house with grass plot in the front, good cellarage and stabling and a large garden at the rear, situated on the east side of the Monmouthshire canal near the Patent Nut and Bolt company. The premises were held for the term of ninety-nine years from the 2nd February 1849 at the ground rent of two pounds ten shillings and six pence.

The next mention of the inn was in the Pontypool Free Press of 3rd October 1890. Dennis Buckley was charged with being drunk and refusing to leave on 6th September. The landlord said the defendant was walking down the canal bank in a state of drink. When the landlady saw him she said she would not allow him in or serve him any beer. The defendant then became very abusive but eventually went home. Since the event he had 'humbly begged pardon' and said it would not happen again. He had been convicted four times before and was fined fifteen shillings.

The article does not give the name of the landlord but on the 1891 census it was George Love who was also a mason. He lived with his wife, Ellen, thirty-four and children – Elizabeth, fourteen, Cornelius, twelve, Esther, nine and William, six. There was also a servant employed – Mary Reardon, seventeen and a boarder, Edward Robbin, thirty-one.

George and Ellen Love were also recorded as being licensees of the inn on the 1901 census. They had only one of their children still living with them, Esther.

George Love had died by 1907 and at Caerleon police court a temporary transfer of the license was granted to 'Miss Love', presumably Esther. However by March 1909 the license had been transferred to Annie Sweeney and Thomas Sweeney.

Thomas and Annie Sweeney were married and on the 1911 census they were aged twenty-eight and twenty-four. They had two children – Eileen, two and May,one. Their niece Annie Chamberlain, ten, was also listed at their premises as was a barmaid, Nellie Love, nineteen.

The next mention of the inn was the 1939 register when the licensee was John Lynch, his wife Mary and daughter also Mary.

In the 1970's it was run by Ray and Doreen Morgan.

The New Bridgend is now closed and boarded up. In December 2019 an application for planning permission was sent to Torfaen Council for the building of homes on the site.

PONTNEWYDD

Cwmbran Gardens Hotel

Cwmbran Gardens Hotel used to be situated on the canal bank between Richmond Place and the recreation ground in Pontnewydd which was also a part of the hotel grounds.

The hotel building was first built as a depot for the Monmouthshire Canal Company but was purchased around 1873 by Richard Clarke, He made an application at Pontypool police court in September of that year for a license for a fruit and recreation garden in Cwmbran. Accompanying him was Mr Alexander Edwards who supported his application and stated the house would be open all week except Sundays. The license was granted.

Described as a 'palace at the disposal of the working man' by the Western Mail, the gates to Mr. Clarke's gardens opened in July 1874. Hundreds visited, mostly working class to whom a few hours in the gardens must have seemed like heaven compared to their work in the mines and other industries. The gardens had been created with no expense spared by Mr. Clarke, a much needed facility that was not bettered anywhere in the county according to the Western Mail who went on to describe the gardens on that opening day as 'elegantly laid out with beds and borders of flowers, rockeries, ferneries, fountains, alcoves and pavilions; also croquet grounds, green lawns and leafy trees for shade. A brook runs nearby crossed with rustic bridges. Exotic plants in hot houses so large they require three to four thousand feet of glass, seven feet wide. A saloon has been fitted up for refreshments. Good order is well preserved and only the well behaved can buy'.

There was also a Turkish bath and concerts held every Thursday evening. In July 1878 a running track was added. The first race was one of a hundred and fifty yards with the first prize of a silver watch. There were seventeen entries.

In September, Mr. Greenway on behalf of Richard Clarke applied for a seven day license. The gardens were open on Sundays as well and attracting around eight hundred visitors. He wanted to be able to provide them with refreshments however the application was refused.

Races at the gardens continued regularly. In October one took place between G. Thomas of Newport and L. James of Swansea. The race attracted a large crowd and Thomas won by few yards. James then accepted a challenge from a spectator from Panteg Steelworks and beat him.

The gardens began to attract all kinds of different entertainment that enticed people from near and far. Hutchinson's and Taylor's Circus gave two performances there in the summer of 1879 which was enjoyed by many but in February 1880, an auction was advertised in the Western Mail for the sale of fruit and ornamental trees from the gardens. The catalogue was said to include thousands of trees and shrubs, some of a rare variety. It seems there had been a depression in trade in the area and it is possibly this reason the plant were sold off. Visitor numbers were also down as an article in the Western Mail of 1880 implies. A fete was held at the gardens on Easter Monday when 'a larger number of persons were present than has been the case since the good times which preceded that depression of trade from which the neighbourhood has suffered recently'.

From this point on the gardens fortunes improved and they became a popular tourist attraction and sporting venue. In November 1882 a race between J. Harrington and J. Cronan of Newport took place. The distance was a hundred and twenty yards with stakes of five pounds a side. Harrington won by a yard and a half.

Richard Clarke died in 1885 but the gardens remained open and were run by his wife and their son, James. Works day trips often visited. In the Weekly Mail of July 1886 it was reported that the employees of Elliot and Jeffrey, proprietors of the Cardiff Engine works visited and also enjoyed dinner provided by Mrs Clarke. It also provided further information about the site. It was set in nine acres of ground and laid out with romantic walks of a mile and a half interspersed with flower beds and tiny fountains. In the mountain stream that ran through the grounds trout fishing was possible.

The following month workmen and friends numbering sixty-five in the employ of Mr. James a builder from Penarth enjoyed a days outing to the gardens where dinner and tea was provided in the hotel by Mrs Clarke. A week later two hundred school children from Nantyglo visited and enjoyed games in the grounds. The children then met in the large hall of the hotel to sing songs and also to thank Mrs Clarke and James for the attention they bestowed upon them.

Cwmbran Gardens Hotel was a very popular attraction but for reasons unknown it was advertised in the property sales of the South Wales Daily News in September 1893. The highest bid it received was £2500, it was withdrawn from sale. It was advertised again in July 1896, this time only receiving bids of £2000, again it was withdrawn.

The site was eventually sold by the end of the 19th century to a Mr Treharne. The 1901 census shows the hotel was split into three separate dwellings called Cwmbran Gardens. The first was occupied by Thomas King, aged forty, his wife Emily also forty and their children – Lily, fifteen, Harry, fourteen, William, thirteen and Ivor, three.

The second dwelling was occupied by Alexander McGregor a thirty-seven year old coal miner and his wife Mary Ellen also thirty-seven. They had three children – John Alexander, nine, Gladys Elsie, eight and Florence Mabel,seven.

The third dwelling was occupied by William Cook, a smelter in the steelworks, aged twenty-nine. With his was his wife Susannah, twenty-four and their children Edith, four and Thomas,two. There was also two of William's brothers – Albert, nineteen and Joel, fourteen plus Abraham Davies, twenty who was a lodger.

It looks as though around this time the hotel and recreation grounds may have become separate entities. In the Pontypool Messenger of 9th March 1907, Mr. Hornby, on behalf of owners Lloyd and Yoreth were looking to remove the license from the hotel to a new premises that was to be situated on the road from Pontnewydd to Upper Cwmbran. It does not mention whether they also owned the recreation grounds but the fact the owners wanted to move the license to a new building showed the interest in Cwmbran Gardens Hotel was fading. Removal of the license at this time though was opposed by the court and not granted.

The last event recorded in the news regarding the gardens was a race between W. Davies of Pontypool and F. Hobby of the Tranch It took place in August 1908 and was a hundred and twenty yards flat race. It created a large amount of local interest as events there always did and Davies won by a yard and a half.

The 1911 census was taken on the night of Sunday April 2nd. It showed the license to Cwmbran Gardens still remained and that it had become a public house. The landlord was William Henry Hodges, aged forty-three. He lived with his wife, Elizabeth, forty-seven. The number of rooms recorded on the census was eight. The Hodges had quite a spacious dwelling for the two of them compared to the eighteen people housed there ten years earlier.

The 1939 register records Valentine Wiggins, fifty-one, living there with his wife, May, fifty.

Cwmbran Gardens went on to become an Ansells pub until it was abandoned and boarded up in the 1960's. All that is left today are the recreation grounds, some fragments of ivy covered wall where the hotel used to be and the street name of Clarke Avenue serving as a reminder of Richard Clarke and his 'palace for the working man'.

Pontnewydd Hotel

We are lucky to know the exact date of the opening of this inn. It was recorded in the Monmouthshire Merlin of 1st September 1855 that a new license was applied for and was granted to William Jones whose house was ready to open by the end of the month. The house was close to

Pontnewydd Station and was to be known as the Pontnewydd Inn. The following year as recorded in the Illustrated Usk Observer of 2nd August, the inn was transferred from William Jones to Thomas Williams. In December 1857 it was transferred again from Thomas Williams to James Stellard.

Soon the inn became a meeting place for the community. In October 1858 a presentation was made there to Mr. Mogford the station master. A large crowd assembled and a dinner was hosted by Mr and Mrs Stellard in the club room to which about fifty people sat down. A gold watch was presented to Mr. Mogford by the Reverend J. Hopkins with a speech focusing on the manner Mr. Mogford carried out his duties. Toasts were given and everyone had an 'agreeable evening'.

In April 1859 a new branch of Oddfellowship opened. It consisted of a large number of members and their dinner was held at the Pontnewydd Inn under the supervision of Brother Thomas. Again in 1860 they held their annual dinner at the inn but in that year the landlord was David Jones.

The inn changed hands again by the time of the 1861 census this time to George Thomas, aged thirty-nine. He lived there with his wife Ann, thirty-nine, daughters May and Emily, aged fifteen and nine and son John, ten. George's father Thomas also lived there. Aged sixty-nine he was employed as a book-keeper. There was also a servant, Ann Phillips, twenty-five.

A few months later in December, George was charged with embezzlement of sixty three pounds twelve shillings and six pence belonging to the overseers of Llanfrechfa Upper. A sum of forty pounds had been acquired by the sale of his goods which had reduced the amount owed to the current amount.

As was usual with most public houses the Pontnewydd Inn was used as a place to hold inquests or to treat the injured. On Monday July 20th 1863 William Highly was travelling by train from Birkenhead to Pontypool station. In Abergavenny he heard the train would be going to Pontrhydyrun and as he lived in Cwmbran decided to get off there. At the station the guard let him and two other men out. William stumbled and fell under the carriage. He was picked up but he was found to have almost severed his leg just below the knee. He also fractured his ankle on the other leg. The flesh on the left side of his face had been taken off by the wheel, leaving his skull exposed. He was taken to the Pontnewydd Inn where he died within a few minutes.

In January 1864 an inquest was held at the inn on the body of Mary Jones. Described as 'aged' she had left the home of her son, with whom she lived, at six o'clock on a Thursday night. At ten o'clock the same night, two lock-men, William and Charles Edwards found her lifeless body in the canal. It was supposed that she had accidentally fallen in.

Landlord George Thomas was in trouble in May 1866 when he had his house open after midnight on the 5th. He pleaded not guilty but the charge was proved and he was fined six shillings and sixpence.

The annual dinner of the Good Intent Lodge of Oddfellows was held in July 1870. A speech was given by collier William Jones. Eighteen months previously he had lost his voice and it had shown no sign of returning. On 22nd July he was at work when his voice suddenly returned. He was 'half demented with joy' reported the Western Mail and ran from place to place proclaiming 'I can speak! I can speak!' At the club dinner he expressed his gratitude to 'Providence'.

By the time of the 1871 census there was a new landlord – William Jones aged sixty-six from Llanfrechfa. He lived with his wife, Annie, forty-nine, and children – William, twenty-two, Annie, nineteen, Thomas, seventeen and Amy, eight. They also rented out a room to Josiah Richards, a photographer.

Concerns were raised by the local government board in December 1871 into the construction of the Pontnewydd sewer under the highway and yard of the inn. A lengthy discussion took place as to whether the premises water supply would be affected in consequence of the sewer being so close to it. An order was made for the work to be carried out anyway but in a way that would safeguard the water.

An inquest was held at the inn in January 1874 on the bodies of Henry Morgan and John Coombs. Both were found drowned in the canal at Five Locks, a place of 'very dangerous character' according to the County Observer. Coombs lodged at the Crosskeys Beerhouse. Morgan was also at the house and left about eight o'clock to go home. The night was very foggy and dark and so it was assumed they walked into the water and died.

A public meeting was held in March 1879 to consider the best course of action to secure the election and that was to form an association for the county which was called the Cwmbran and Pontnewydd Branch of the Monmouthshire Liberal Association.

On January 18th 1881 William Jones died and the inn was taken over by Thomas Williams, forty-one, of Pontnewydd and his wife Elizabeth. With them lived their six children – Charles,fifteen, Annie, fourteen, Kate, twelve, Edith,ten, Frederick, six, and Thomas, two. There also a servant Elizabeth Wilkes aged sixteen.

A quiet period followed as there was little mention of the inn in the news until August 1887 when a meeting of Liberals was held there. An address was given by Mr. Mark Lewis and Mr. Henry Parfitt moved a resolution declaring satisfaction at the recent Liberal successes and confidence in Mr. Gladstone and his Home Rule policy.

By 1890 the Pontnewydd Inn had become the Pontnewydd Hotel and Thomas Haynes, forty-three, was landlord. He lived with his wife Jane, thirty-eight and children – Alice,eight, Ethel, six and Arthur, three.

In January 1890 Martin Edwards held an inquest regarding the death of John Griffin aged thirty-eight. He lived at the Square in Upper Cwmbran with his wife Louisa who said she last saw him alive sat by a table. She went to visit her mother and upon her return found him hanging by some twine around his neck fastened to a beam. The jury returned a verdict of suicide while temporarily insane.

In June 1890 workmen from Panteg, Avondale, Tynewydd, Patent Nut and Bolt and Henllys works met to consider the appointment of a medical man by the end of the year.

Thomas Haynes was involved in a horse and trap accident in December 1890. He was driving down the Pitch near Lower Pontnewydd station when his trap collided with another vehicle going in the opposite direction. The horse ran wildly towards the hotel. The driver, Isaiah Gough was badly shaken and the horse 'ruined'.

Another inquest was held at the hotel in January 1893. Mr. Moses Roberts Jones led an investigation into the deaths of Thomas Morgan, timber-man aged forty-eight and Frederick John Hamlin referred to by the Evening Express as a 'boy'. Both were killed at Cwmbran Colliery. Mark Hamlin, the boy's father said his son was thirteen. Mark was late for work on the day in question. John was already in the mine. Mark went in and called out to him to which John answered 'Hello father'. Mark noticed that about five or six tons of roof had fallen. He could see his son was under the fall and so ran for help. When the boy was rescued he had died.

John Morgan, the brother of Thomas Morgan said Thomas was married with five children and had worked underground all his life. A verdict of accidental death was delivered.

In August 1893 a meeting of tin plate workers union met at the hotel. Mr. George Freeman presided over a 'fair number of delegates' it was reported in the South Wales Daily News of 21st August.

At the beginning of the 20th century and on the 1901 census Thomas Haynes and family still occupied the Pontnewydd Hotel.

The first news story of the new century was reported in the Western Mail of 2nd September 1905. It concerned a mass meeting of workmen employed at the Upper Cwmbran colliery. On the agenda was the 'non-unionist' question which had been causing dissatisfaction with the workmen. The following resolution was passed – 'That this meeting of workmen pledges itself to do all in its power to get every man outside the pale of the organization to join the same. Failing this, within the coming month that more stringent measures be taken to compel them to come and join the same'.

Thomas Haynes and family had left the hotel by 1911. The census recorded Walter Walker, thirty-four and his wife Alice, twenty-eight living there.

The Pontnewydd Inn closed in 2012 the following year it was damaged by fire. Today it has been renovated but still remains closed.

Oddfellows Arms

The 'Oddies' was built in the mid 1860's. Its name derives from the Oddfellows Society which was formed to help those less fortunate. On the top of its logo are three links representing friendship, love and truth. Symbols were important in the early days of these societies as many people were unable to read.

The first occupants of the property were the Evans family. Recorded on the 1871 census, William Evans, forty, an engine fitter lived there with his wife Sarah, thirty-seven and niece Christiana Dutton. There were also two boarders, John Thomas, thirty-two and Benjamin Davies, twenty-seven.

An article from the Monmouthshire Merlin gives a glimpse of the environmental conditions in Pontnewydd in 1871. At the Llanfrechfa local board meeting Vicar J Jenkins addressed the issue of an impure water supply. In the summer of 1870 an inspector had compiled a report after an outbreak of Enteric Fever or Typhoid Fever. This would have been caused by Salmonella bacteria from human bodily waste entering the water supply. Analysis of the water from a pump at Ladywell Road showed it unfit for consumption. An order was given for a new pump to be placed in positions free from pollution and a culvert to be continued from the corner of the Oddfellows into a field. Property owners were encouraged to connect drains to it to empty their 'privies'.

The following month William Evans along with George Rich were charged with assaulting Cornelius Connolly. The case for Connolly was only supported by his own evidence and that of P.C. Burrows. Mr. Greenway for the defence called a number of witnesses to show that it was Connolly who was the aggressor and that Burrows was lying. The bench decided the assault by Rich was more aggravated than a blow justified. He was fined forty shillings. The charge against Evans was dismissed.

February 1878 saw the death of one of the oldest inhabitants of Pontnewydd – John Williams. He was the deacon of Bethel Independent chapel and one of the founders of the Good Intent Lodge of Oddfellows in Pontnewydd.

William Evans was summoned in March 1878 for assaulting Eli Hodgeson of Newport. On the 1st, Hodgeson went to the Oddfellows to collect a payment concerning some gas fittings. Evans refused to pay and called him a 'swindler' before throwing him out. The bench dismissed the case.

By October 1878 Sarah Evans had taken over the running of the inn from her husband. At police court in March 1879 Phillip Willmott, who did not appear, was charged with trespass by breaking windows on October 26th 1878. Sarah said that he broke in to her house breaking the 'bow-window'. She stated it cost her seven shillings and six pence to have it repaired. Willmott was summoned at the time but he absconded. On hearing he was back in the area she took out another summons. He was fined twenty shillings.

On the 1881 census Sarah Evans was the head of the household however the household consisted only of her and a servant, Mary Thomas who worked there as a waitress. She was also her niece.

In 1882 Sarah Evans decided to leave the Oddfellows. An advertisement was published in the South Wales Daily News in May – 'to let, the whole of a good garden planted with kidney, potatoes, onions and a large stock of fruit trees, raspberries, strawberries and also eight hives of bees'. Then in July the house was advertised – 'to let, this capital house. Present tenant the only occupier for sixteen years. A good trade doing and good reasons for giving up'.

The next mention of the Oddfellows was on the 1891 census. Thomas Haynes, also of the Pontnewydd Inn, was landlord. In February Haynes was charged with selling drink to a drunken man and permitting drunkenness on his premises. At about eight o'clock at night Michael Bush and his wife entered the inn, walked through the house and into the kitchen where Mrs Haynes was sitting by the fire. Mr Haynes was attending to the bar. Mrs Bush asked for a drink and was served. About forty-five minutes later P.C. Jones visited and found Michael Bush in an intoxicated state. He was standing up but another man was supporting him. Mrs Bush told her husband to go home but he refused, not until he had another quart of beer. Mrs Haynes refused to serve him. Mrs Bush was advised not to let her husband have anymore so she took the glass off him and drank it herself. Mr Bush then got up and staggered away with his wife. Mr Haynes was then told he should not have served him to which Mrs Haynes replied that it was not his drink anyway it was his wife's. Bush was fined seven shillings and six pence.

By the time of the 1911 census Llewellyn Williams, forty-eight, was landlord. He lived with his wife – Susie, twenty-nine and children, Reginald, eight, Ronald, six and Minnie, eleven months. The Oddfellows is still open today.

Old Bridgend Inn

The first mention of the Old Bridgend (or the Bridge Inn as it was known) was in January 1856 when Mary Morgan was charged with keeping her house open between three and five o clock on a Sunday afternoon. She was fined ten shillings plus nine shillings costs.

In November 1857 Mary Herbert lived there. She gave evidence at the trial of Mr James Greenland, a letter carrier for Newport post office. He called at the inn to buy a brandy and was accused of cashing a cheque that was not his. He was later cleared of any wrongdoing.

On 30th February 1861 the body of a man named Samuel Fox, twenty-four, the son of Mrs England was found floating in the canal between Pontnewydd and Five Locks. An inquest was held at the inn and a verdict of found drowned was returned.

Mrs England was Ann England, aged forty-eight on the 1861 census. Her husband William, forty was a coal miner. They had one other son Robert England, aged seventeen and also employed a servant, Jane Thomas aged eighteen.

John Lewis occupied the inn on the 1871 census with his wife Louise, twenty-five. They had one daughter, Eliza, aged one. John's sister-in -law also lived there, Margaret Williams,aged eighteen.

By November 1871 Mr. Leo was landlord. He was convicted of permitting drunkenness and keeping a disorderly house. Mr. Smythe who appeared in court for Leo said he was a 'respectable innkeeper and a conviction might cause problems when renewing his license' His appeal though was dismissed with costs.

Lydia Upham was charged with refusing to leave the inn on 7th August 1878. Anne Baker was the landlady who was also charged with assaulting Lydia on the same date. It appeared that Lydia's husband had been in the inn and she was there to order him home. When he refused to go Lydia took a glass of rum off the table and threw it away. She then became abusive and violent. Anne, it was alleged hit Lydia who was eventually thrown out. Lydia was fined ten shillings and Anne fifteen shillings.

The Bakers also became bankrupt in August 1878. The inn was sold by auction on 31st May 1879. It was described in the Pontypool Free Press as a 'freehold property with double front shop and cottage premises in the occupation of Thomas Williams and other tenants, comprising bar, tap room, bar parlour, sitting room, kitchen, four bedrooms, cottage yard, gardens and frontage of eighty feet'.

Thomas Williams became landlord of the Bridgend as well as the Pontnewydd Inn. The inn now though was known as the Bridge End Hotel.

In November 1881 a tragic accident occurred. Patrick Reardon aged eight, was riding in a boat as it was rising in a lock opposite the inn. He fell into the water and it appeared he had been left there for some time due to the 'inhuman conduct' of boatman Joseph Saunders who, while aware the boy had fallen in drove his boat away without offering any assistance. An inquest was held at the inn by Mr. Brewer, the boatman was not present. The boy's little brother was sworn in and said his brother fell off the boat and the boy who was steering tried to reach him but couldn't. The boat then went up the canal. A witness, Kate Driscoll ran after the boatman who informed her that the boy was in the lock. The jury gave a verdict of accidental death but the boatman was severely reprimanded for inhuman conduct.

In April 1883, landlord Thomas William's son Charles, aged 17, committed suicide by shooting himself with a revolver. Charles had been ill for two weeks but had no symptoms that would have led his parents to believe he would kill himself. Thomas had been sitting up all night with him and fell asleep about 5.30 a.m. Shortly afterwards Charles jumped out of bed, grabbed a revolver that was in the room and shot himself through the heart. The noise woke Thomas who found him dead at his feet.

Thomas Williams was still landlord on the 1891 census though he was by this time a widower living with his children. The family continued to reside at the Bridge End into the early twentieth century and were also recorded on the 1901 census.

It was all change for the 1911 census. The Bridge End was still a hotel but it was run by Edward Lloyd, forty-six and wife Mary, thirty-seven. They had four children – Harold, fifteen, Cecilia, thirteen, Albert, ten and Frederick, five. Also on the census return was George Smith, twenty-four and a boarder, Rowland Harrison, seventeen and Beatrice Gooding, a 19 year old servant.

On the 1939 register the Bridge End was run by Edwin B Thomas, sixty-one and wife Sarah, sixty-six and is still open today.

Cross Keys

Using the census enumerator's route, the original Cross Keys pub was situated between Ty Pwca cottage and the lock-keeper's cottage, also known as Canal Cottage in Five Locks.

On the 1861 census it was occupied by John Makeley, forty-four who only gave his profession as that of a coal miner. He lived with his wife Sarah, forty-two and sons William, eighteen and George, fifteen.

At the time of the 1871 census it was known as the Cross Keys Beerhouse. Again its occupier, Robert Hart, thirty, only gives one occupation, that of a bolt-maker. He lived there with his wife Emma, twenty-five and son William, two.

We know that drink was being served there in the mid 1870s from an article in the Monmouthshire Merlin of June 1874 when David Davies was charged with being drunk and refusing to leave. He was fined ten shillings or ten days in prison. He chose the latter.

The Cross Keys made the news in March 1883 when James Thatcher, a brewer's haulier from Newport was summoned for leaving a horse and cart unattended. Constable Davies gave evidence in support of the charge stating the horse and cart were unattended outside the inn for twenty minutes. Mr Greenway, solicitor, appeared for the defendant and said he had not left it for longer than needed. He had worked at the Castle Brewery for many years and had never been complained about. The bench said it would deal leniently with him.

By the 1901 census the Cross Keys was run by Thomas Jones, aged thirty-five, a hammer-man as well as publican. He lived with wife Harriet and daughters Ethel, nine, Dorothy, five, Elsie, four and Gladys, two. They also had a one year old son, Ernie.

The Cross Keys was a five roomed property with seven people already living in it. It is unknown whether the Jones family still occupied the pub in 1907 but what is known was that it took in lodgers. One of these, Frank Rowlands, thirty-three, was found drowned in the canal in November of that year. He was seen in Pontnewydd late at night and it was supposed while crossing a lock he fell in the water. He was found with two cuts on his head assumed to have been caused by hitting the stonework.

Betting was causing a concern at the Cross Keys in September 1908. Edgar Bowen from Pontypool was summoned for visiting a public place for the purpose of betting. P.C. Hughes stated he saw two men reading a sporting paper on the canal bank between the Cross Keys and Cwmbran Gardens. They then wrote on slips of paper and when Bowen appeared he was handed something by one of the men. P.C. Hughes followed Bowen to the Cross Keys and told him he was arresting him on suspicion of betting on the canal bank. He was taken to the police station and was found to have the sum of eleven pounds, three shillings and two and a half pence. There was nothing found however to suggest he had been betting and the case was dismissed.

William Nicholas was landlord in 1911. He was forty-one, single with no family. In January of that year he was summoned to Pontypool court for selling alcohol on Christmas Day during prohibited hours. Two friends, Ivor Morgan and John Hibbs were also charged with being drunk on the premises. P.C. Hughes gave evidence that around ten in the morning he heard a commotion from inside the house. When the landlord opened the door he saw the two men sitting by a table with glasses half full of beer and some empty bottles. When questioned the landlord said the two had stayed at the house until stop tap on Christmas Eve then later returned to sing carols. They were not drinking alcohol merely ginger brandy and lemonade. The court erupted into laughter as the two were asked if they had sung

'While Policemen Watched'. All were fined twenty shillings.

There were two families living at 'Cross Keys' on the 1939 register. Paul Forrester, sixty and a bricklayer. His wife was Rose, sixty-six. The second occupants were Clifford Jenkins, thirty-seven and a crane driver. His wife was Florence, 31.

This Cross Keys Inn was probably demolished with the building of new houses in the area with a new Cross Keys replacing it. This too is closed now and has been converted into a private home.

The Terrace Inn

The first mention of the Terrace Inn appears to be in the Monmouthshire Merlin on 4th February 1865. Mr. Brewer, coroner held an inquest there on the body of a newborn child belonging to Jemima Evans. She lived with and worked as a house-keeper to a carpenter with the same surname who also lived in the neighbourhood. A woman called to see her but Jemima complained of feeling unwell. Later the woman returned with another woman. They found Jemima in her bed having just given birth. They discovered the baby was dead and had been placed in another room wrapped in a shawl. Dr. Cousins carried out a post mortem and the jury returned a verdict of stillborn.

In April 1870 a Mr J. Graham was offering for sale by public auction at the inn on Friday May 6th, five freehold properties. This consisted of four dwelling houses with 'good gardens and piggeries'. At the time the properties were occupied by 'Jarrett, Miles, Evans and James' families. The weekly rent was three shillings and six pence. The fifth property auctioned was the 'double licensed house with good garden' called the Terrace Inn. The five properties were 'prettily situated' adjoining the parish road and in good repair.

On the 1871 census Elizabeth Jenkins, forty was landlady. She lived with her daughter Kate, twelve and sons William, eleven and John, four. Elizabeth continued to be landlady on the 1881 census. Her husband was recorded on this one as William Jenkins, a fifty-two year old coal merchant. Only one child remained at home – John and a servant was employed – sixteen year old Ann Davies.

Elizabeth Jenkins continued to be landlady for both the 1891 and 1901 censuses. Her son John remained at home working as a barman.

The Terrace made the news in February 1904. John Henry Williams, a grocer of Pontrhydyrun was summoned by the Inland Revenue for selling tobacco without a license. On the 14th November, Mr. Nicholls of the Inland Revenue saw a haulier deliver fifty packets of cigarettes and a pound of tobacco to the Terrace Inn. The defendant said it was a 'technical offence' and appealed to the bench to take into account the time he had spent on Newport Council. He was fined forty shillings.

On the 1911 census the inn was recorded to have eleven rooms and Elizabeth's son, John had become the landlord. Also recorded were two nephews – William George Moseley, twenty-seven and Charles Campbell Moseley, sixteen.

The inn was next mentioned on the 1939 register. Herbert Iggulden, fifty-three, resided there with wife Phillipa, forty-five and sons Kenneth, twenty-two and Phillip, thirteen.

In recent years the inn was called Fairces but has now returned to its original name.

Kings Head

In September 1865 at Caerleon petty sessions a license was granted to George Stewart to sell intoxicating drinks at a house then known as King's Head Gardens.

George Stewart was a gardener and his premises were likened to that of the nearby Cwmbran Gardens Hotel. On the 1871 census he was forty-six years old and lived with his wife, Mary, forty and children – Margaret, seventeen, Elizabeth, sixteen, James, thirteen, Richard, eleven, John, nine, Henry, seven, George, four and Ann, one.

The King's Head was mentioned in the County Observer newspaper of 4 September 1875. It was mentioned in licensing sessions as being a fully licensed house 'at which there were also pleasure grounds but everyone must confess Mr Clarke's grounds were infinitely superior'.

In October 1876 an inquest was held by Mr. Brewer on the death of an almost naked man whose body was found in the Afon Llwyd river on 1st October. No one came forward to identify the body that lay at the King's Head. No one knew where it had come from or how it got there. No one was missing a relative either. The man was aged twenty-five to thirty years old, of medium height with 'dark sandy whiskers'. He had a broad flat nose and was wearing moleskin trousers and working boots.

George Stewart and family were still living at the King's Head for the 1881 census where the children were helping out with the business. Daughter, Margaret was a barmaid while Richard was a gardener.

By October 1889 the Stewarts had left and William Wells was landlord. That month Silas Edworthy, an engine driver from Croesyceiliog was charged with being drunk and refusing to leave the premises. Mr. Webb prosecuted. Neither defendant appeared. Mr Webb stated Wells had good reason to eject Edworthy. On Saturday night about 9.30 p.m. Edworthy came to the house drunk and demanding beer 'On strap'. Wells refused to serve him and asked him to leave. Edworthy offered to pay for his beer but Wells still refused. Edworthy then used abusive language and Wells went to escort him out. Edworthy lost his balance and fell down to the floor pulling Wells on top of him. While he was on the ground another man named Bevan rushed up and hit Wells. Edworthy then went back in the building and Wells had to get him out all over again. Edworthy and Bevan were both fined twenty shillings each.

On the 1891 census, William Wells was thirty-nine years old and his occupation was given as 'hotel keeper'. He lived with his wife, Elizabeth, thirty-six and children, William, seventeen, Amelia, sixteen, George, thirteen, Elizabeth, eight and Gertrude, six.

In December 1891 an inquest was held at the King's Head by E. Davies, deputy coroner, regarding the death of Thomas Morgan, aged seventy-five, a hay dealer from Crosskeys. On the night of his death he had been feeling unwell on his way to Pontnewydd railway station. He later dropped dead in the road. The jury returned a verdict of death by natural causes.

The members of Pontnewydd Black Watch Football Club sat down to a meal provided by Mr. Wells in April 1892. The King's Head was its club headquarters. Songs were sung by W. Saunders, C. Wood, J. Brown, Thomas Hodges and R. Phelps with Mr. Bumford on piano. Toasts were given after which everyone sang the National Anthem.

By May 1909 William Wells had left the King's Head. He lived at Durban Place, Pontnewydd. One evening as he was going to bed he fell downstairs and sustained such injuries that he died shortly after. It was thought he may have had a fit.

William Wells's son, William took over the running of the hotel. He was living there at the time of the 1911 census, aged thirty-seven. With him was his sister in law, Mary Matthews, forty-two and servant Emma Matthews, twenty-one.

The 1939 register showed Vernon Jenkins, fifty-five was landlord. He lived with wife, Beatrice, forty-seven and also hotel assistant and children Arnold, twenty-three and Beatrice, seventeen. There was also an evacuee, Lilian Lewis, twenty-eight carrying out unpaid domestic duties.

In the 1980's an upstairs room was used as a dance studio for the Johnson School of Dancing. The inn then changed its name to the Oriental Garden but today it is closed though renovations are taking place at the time of writing.

CROESYCEILIOG

Upper Cock Inn

Croesyceiliog translated means 'The Cross of the Cock' and may refer to a large crowing cock that used to stand in a field near the inn. The sculpture was thought to have been destroyed by Cromwellian troops in the 17th century. The inn once had a sign outside which read -

'Here is a tavern, the Cross of the Cock

A welcome to each one for his penny

Good ale to all for payment

Come in, you can taste it'

The inn's name could also derive from the 'cock' horses which used to transport heavy loads up hills.

The Upper Cock is an ancient building. We know it existed in 1839 as the Chartists stopped here on their way to Newport from Pontypool. It was a rainy night and their gunpowder damp so they tried to dry it in the inn's ovens. The visit of the Chartists is well documented for the Lower Cock, we can only assume it was similar for the Upper Cock.

On the 1851 census the inn was known as the Upper Cross. It was occupied by Samuel Davis, forty-five, his wife, Rachel, forty, sister-in-law, Eleanor Williams, twenty-six and herself also an innkeeper. They employed one servant, Ann Price, twenty-one.

The name Upper Cock inn does not appear on the 1861 or 1871 census and on the 1881 census there is only a reference to a 'Croesyceiliog Inn'. This was the home of William Williams, sixty-three, wife Mary, fifty-five, son, William, fifteen and servant Mary Pritchard, twenty-five.

Finally on the 1891 census the inn is referred to as the Upper Cock, George Mostam, thirty-eight, was the landlord. He lived there with his wife, Mary, aged fifty-six and son George, fourteen. They employed a servant, Mary Davis, sixteen.

The 1901 Kelly's Business Directory gives Abram Bevan as landlord at this time but on the census it is his widow, Mary Jane, thirty-six who took over and became landlady.

At a licensing meeting in Caerleon in February 1905, magistrates objected to the renewal of the license but this was a temporary decision as in the 'wanted' advertisements of the Evening Express in December 1909, the landlord, Mr. Jones was looking for a 'good, strong, general servant'.

It was all change again for the 1911 census where Benjamin Lewis Jones was landlord. He resided with his wife, Ada, forty-one, son William, ten and daughter Margery, nine. They also employed a nineteen year old servant called Agnes Hopkins. The 1911 census also records that the inn had twelve rooms.

On the 1939 register the inn was occupied by Jesse and Rachel Freeman aged fifty-five and fifty-eight years old. Today it is the only original public house left in Croesyceiliog out of four.

Lower Cock Inn

The Lower Cock Inn was situated on the Highway in Croesyceiliog where the Tewdric Court bungalows are today. It is unclear when it was built but it did play a part in the Chartist uprising of 4th November 1839.

It has generally been accepted in local lore that it was the nearby Upper Cock Inn that played hosts to the chartists however an article in the South Wales Daily News from 21 April 1877 which reproduced letters written by one of the leaders, Zephaniah Williams, tells a different story.

At the time of the Chartists march on Newport the Lower Cock Inn was kept by Mrs Glazebrook. For three days previous the inn had been exhibiting a boy from Carmarthenshire, probably to attract customers. He was thirteen years old and known as the 'Porcupine Boy' due to him being covered in wart-like scales all over his body. After his departure the village of Croesyceiliog returned to normal, blissfully unaware of the events that were about to unfold.

The night of the march was 'wet, dark and miserable'. The only customer in the Lower Cock was a man named Absalom from Pembrokeshire. The landlady's son had gone to bed leaving his mother to close up the house.

Not long afterwards a man named Barnabas, a brewer from Pontypool arrived along with another man named Thomas Watkins, also from Pontypool. They knocked and asked where 'Glazebrook' was, explaining that their horses were 'completely knocked up' but as Glazebrook the son was in bed they decided they would try to carry on a bit further with their journey. They next arrived at the Upper Cock Inn and called to the landlord Joe Davis. They left their horses there, had a few drinks then left to walk to Pontypool.

The first group of chartists marched through Croesyceiliog without stopping. Mrs Glazebrook was now in her bedroom. She was undressed and ready to go to sleep until she heard a knock on the door. A man shouted 'Glazebrook' a couple of times so she in response shouted from her bedroom window. 'Who's there'. It was so dark though and the rain so heavy she could barely see. Her son heard her shouting and decided it was 'probably some old customer from the hills'.

Eventually Mrs Glazebrook received a reply. The voice said 'a friend from the Varteg who wants a quart of beer'. She replied 'Well if you drink it quickly you shall have a quart of beer' She put on a gown, went downstairs, opened the door and handed the man a jug. 'Let me come in a minute out of the rain' he continued but as soon as he had set foot inside it was obvious he was not alone as a number of other men rushed in with him. Hearing the commotion Mrs Glazebrook's son jumped out of bed, hurriedly got dressed and ran downstairs to find the inn full of rain drenched men. 'Hello' he said 'What is up my lads? Where are you all going to?' 'To Newport' they told him he observed a man named Parry held a stable pike in his hand 'What are you going to do with that?' he asked. 'This is to turn them over' was the reply.

The chartists then insisted that fires should be lit in all of the rooms. Mr Glazebrook needed to get coal for this and on going out through the back door to get some observed an array of pikes, scythes and knives fastened to the end of long sticks He eventually learned of the Chartist rising and realised his house was full of them.

After warming themselves and drinking freely the chartists quietly went on their way. Not long after another group arrived demanding drink. Mr Glazebrook thought it wise to be civil and be as obliging as possible and in return the chartists acted the same. Some of them decided to seek refuge at the inn. 'They took me as I was going to chapel' said one. 'And I as I was eating my supper' said another. Some hid themselves in the cellar, others in the bedrooms until it was safe to escape and return to their homes.

At six o clock the following morning, Jones the Watchmaker, dressed in a black suit, walked into the Lower Cock. He asked for a glass of brandy and sat down. Mr Glazebrook approached him. 'It appears' he said 'that you are one of the leaders of this chartist affair; depend upon it if so, you will either be hanged or transported'. 'Do you think so?' asked Jones. 'Yes' was the reply 'for this going to Newport is a wrong idea altogether'.

At that point some more men arrived and on seeing Jones exclaimed while holding a blunderbuss to his ear 'Jones! Damn me if he hasn't turned traitor. You should have been in Newport hours ago. If you don't come at once I'll blow your brains out' So Jones jumped up and left. As the gang followed one of them grabbed Mr Glazebrook and tried dragging him along with them only releasing him after his protests that he needed to look after his mother.

On their return from Newport the chartists again called at the Lower Cock. They were wet, tired and their spirits were broken. A tragedy would have occurred there and then had it not been for Mr Glazebrook who stopped the attempts of the chartists to dry their wet gunpowder by the fire.

The Lower Cock was listed on the 1841 census. Anne Glazebrook, or Glasbrook as it was spelled by the enumerator, was fifty-five and her son Edward was twenty-five. By the time of the next census in 1851, Edward was the head of the house, his mother having presumably died. He was married to Eliza, thirty-two and had four children – Frederick,eleven, Anne, seven, Sarah, five and John, fifteen months. A servant was also employed. Her name was Sarah James and she was twenty-five.

The Lower Cock changed hands by 1871. The landlord on the census for that year was John Powell aged sixty-five. His wife Sarah was seventy. They had two daughters assisting them in running the inn – Catherine aged thirty-three and Anne, thirty-one. Ten years later on the next census Catherine was the landlady. She was unmarried and living with her was her seventeen year old niece, Clara Powell and her four year old nephew, John Arthur Day. To help with the running of the inn Mary Jane Jones, seventeen was employed as a servant.

It was all change again for the 1891 census. Catherine Matthews, forty-four, was landlady. She was single and employed a servant, Harriet Love, seventeen and also rented a room to boarder Walter Strong.

Into the 20th century, Mary Ann Yendoll a thirty year old widow was landlady .She lived with her daughters – Violet, twelve and Dorothy, four. Her sister Agnes Murray, nineteen, worked as a barmaid and a servant, Helen Powell, seventeen was also employed. These were possibly the last people to run the inn because in March 1904 the license for the Lower Cock was refused as it was deemed no longer necessary. The Lower Cock ceased to exist as an inn and the building fell into disrepair.

In February 1905, a Mr Corner submitted plans in court for the rebuilding of the inn but after deliberation the justices rejected them.

The Lower Cock was still inhabited as a dwelling though. The 1911 census shows John Sprake, forty, living there with his family – wife, Susan, thirty-eight and children John, fifteen, James, fourteen, Dorothy, fourteen, Howard, ten and Ida, three. John and his son John both worked in the iron foundry while James was a grocer's assistant.

The Lower Cock continued to be used as a dwelling until the mid 20th century. On the 1939 register there was a dwelling called Lower Cross House which was probably it. It was occupied by Fred and Alice Austin aged thirty-eight and thirty-six but it would not survive for much longer as it was swept away by the plans for a new town and as mentioned before, Tewdric Court now stands on its site.

Cambrian Inn

This inn was situated at the Garw, Croesyceiliog. It seems to have been a very quiet pub as the lack of stories in old newspapers suggests.

It was recorded on the 1851 census as being occupied by seventy year old William Williams. He lived with his wife, Florence, aged fifty-six and children – John, thirty-five, Hannah, twenty-eight, Isaac, twenty-three and Eliza, twenty-one. They also employed a servant, Anne Absalom aged twenty-six.

On the 1861 census Florence Williams was the landlady having taken over after the death of her husband. Only her son John was recorded on the census however there was a servant, Matilda Davies, seventeen and a lodger, Samuel Crew, sixty-nine. Also recorded was a visitor to the inn, Gertrude Benson probably a family member as she was unlikely to have visited by herself at three years old.

By the 1881 census the inn had passed to Ephraim Davies, seventy-four and his wife Ann, sixty-nine. They employed a servant, Ann Rees, twenty-seven.

It was all change again for the 1891 census. George Day, forty-one was the landlord. He was also employed as a bricklayer. He lived with wife, Ann, forty-six and sons Arthur, fourteen and George, twelve. On the night of the census a visitor was recorded who was probably a family member, Walter Day, thirty-eight.

In August 1900 at a meeting of the Pontypool Rural District Council, an inspector reported that he had written to a company called Phillips and Sons of Newport, informing them that there was no objection to a urinal being constructed at the Cambrian Inn as long as there was proper drainage and it was cemented so as not to cause a nuisance. There had been no epidemics in the area to the best of his knowledge.

George Day had died by the time of the 1901 census so his wife, Ann took on the role of landlady. Her two sons were still at home with her as well as servant Amelia Jones, seventeen.

William King of Pontnewydd appeared at Cwmbran police court on April 1904. On the 7th of the month he had gone to the inn on the off-chance of meeting James Dommett who had been to Usk sessions to give evidence in a licensing case against the Lower Cock. After 'pecking' at Dommett for giving evidence, King challenged him to a fight outside then hit him in the eyes and nose. A police officer stated that Dommett's nose bled so much that two buckets of water were discoloured. King was fined two pounds or a month in prison.

Ann Day, now almost seventy, was still landlady on the 1911 census. She employed a servant, Margaret Rowlands, aged sixteen. Her son George was recorded as a visitor along with his wife, Lily. They had one child but it had died. Also recorded was the number of rooms at the inn which was seven.

On the 1939 register the inn was run by Alfred Harris, fifty-one with his wife, May, thirty-six. There was also a son registered, Malcolm, two.

After the Harrises the inn was again run by the Day family. Then in the 1950's by Fred and Alice Austin. The Cambrian was demolished around the late 1960's

Royal Oak

The Royal Oak was recorded on the 1841 census when it was occupied by John Thomas, fifty-five and his wife Mary, sixty.

On the 1851 census William Morgan, sixty-one lived there with his wife, Mary, seventy-two. William was employed both as a carpenter and a beer house keeper. A servant was also employed, Sarah Carter, nineteen. The Morgans were also recorded on the 1861 census along with their daughter, Agnes, forty-three.

James Leonard Knapp was the landlord in December 1872. He was listed in the Monmouthshire Merlin as his business had gone into liquidation. By February 1873 he was declared bankrupt. On 28th February of that year the Monmouthshire Merlin announced a sale by auction on Monday March 3rd. It gave a comprehensive list of what was to be sold, room by room -

Kitchen – mahogany table, two settles, six chairs, an eight day clock, fender and fire irons, six pictures with hunting scenes.

Sitting room – sofa, three chairs, chest of drawers, five pictures, easy chair, Pier glass, clock, corner cupboard, glasses, lamp, chimney ornaments.

Bedroom 1 – fender and fire irons, iron bedstead, two mattresses, feather bed, sheets, blankets, counterpane, carpeting, commode.

Bedroom 2 – fender and fire irons, two bedsteads, two mattresses, swing glass, two feather-beds, sheets, blankets, counterpane, carpeting.

Bedroom 3 – bedstead, mill puff bed, mattresses, sheets, blankets, quilts, glass stand, table and chair.

Smoking room – seven chairs, clock, sofa, six pictures, fender and fire irons, chimney ornaments.

There is no mention of the Royal Oak Inn on the 1881 census only Royal Oak cottages. It was mentioned on the 1891 census when Hannah Watkins, a widow aged fifty-eight lived there with her children – Thomas, thirty-two, Susan, twenty-nine, Annie, nineteen, William, eighteen, Thomas five, William, one and grand-daughter Sarah, five.

Thomas Watkins took over the Royal Oak on the 1901 census probably because Hannah had died. He lived with his wife Susan, thirty-nine, and children – Tom, thirteen and employed as a cattle-man, William, eleven, John, eight and Alfred, three.

The Watkins family still lived at the inn on the 1911 census though the property is just known as Royal Oak and Thomas Watkins's profession is that of a chair-maker in the ironworks. There were two more children recorded – Charles, nine and Hilda, three. The 1911 census also states the Royal Oak had only four rooms whereas when it was auctioned in 1873 it had more.

The Royal Oak was still around for the 1939 register, occupied by widower Isaac Turner, eighty-two and sons William, fifty-two and Alfred, fifty.

The Royal Oak was demolished. The closest site to its location is in the name Royal Oak Green, Croesyceiliog.

LLANTARNAM

The Coopers Arms

The Coopers Arms was situated in a row of cottages on Abbey Lane said to date from the 18th century. In the early 1800's the inn was run by the Farrant family. On the 1841 census John Farrant was recorded as being a carpenter living with his wife Ann and daughter, Ann.

On the 1851 census John Farrant, thirty-nine gave his occupation as a master carpenter and innkeeper. He and Ann had two children listed – Mary Ann, ten and Louisa, three. There was another John Farrant at the inn employed as a servant, and also a sixteen year old apprentice, William Durbin and a lodger, Dennis Cogan from Ireland.

On 23rd September 1854 the Loyal Llantarnam Abbey Lodge was opened by two of the Blaenavon district officers, Brother William Waters and Brother Joseph Kay. Twenty-two members were initiated and afterwards Brother Kay delivered a speech on the moral principles arising from societies such as these for benevolent purposes. The new lodge then sat down to supper.

In December of the same year the members of Lodge 40, Merthyr and district also met at the Coopers Arms. They subscribed ten shillings towards the Patriotic fund.

Members of the Humanity Lodge celebrated their fourth anniversary on 30th June 1856. They formed a procession and walked to Pentre Bach Farm and then to the Coopers Arms where they were entertained and given refreshments by Brother Thomas before returning to their lodge room.

In July 1857 Joseph Pain and Luke Thomas were charged with stealing from Joseph Sawtell, a bag of bran. Sawtell had missed property previously and so employed Thomas Wood to watch his premises. On 9th June, Wood and the two prisoners were drinking in the Coopers Arms. On leaving Thomas asked for some bran. Pain borrowed a quantity of bran from a nearby mill, leaving it in the kitchen. The bran was found in Thomas's house two days later. A jury found Wood not guilty. Thomas was acquitted but Pain had twelve months in prison.

The inn was advertised in March 1858 as 'to be let with immediate possession' and was described as an 'old established inn'.

The next recorded landlord was Thomas Watkins. In August 1864 he was charged with allowing drunkenness and disorderly behaviour on his premises. He was fined twenty shillings plus nine shillings and six pence costs.

James Edwards was the landlord in 1869. In May of that year he was charged with having his house open during prohibited hours. P.C. Burroughs said that he saw four men and a woman inside. Even though all were sober Edwards was fined forty shillings.

James Edwards was still at the Coopers Arms on the 1871 census. He was fifty-three years old at this time and lived with his wife, Catherine, fifty-one, daughter Catherine Williams, twenty-six, sons John, twenty-four and George twenty-one and daughters Elizabeth, fifteen and Louisa, seven.

The inn went through a quiet period as no news stories could be found during the 1870's. James Edwards still ran the inn on the 1881 census with his wife Catherine. Only the youngest daughter Louisa still lived with them.

In November 1882 and inquest was held at the inn on the body of Thomas Hayes of Caerleon who had died at Llantarnam police station. A huge thunderstorm had raged on the evening he died. Hayes had been walking from Cwmbran to his house. Around 9.30 pm he was found unconscious on the road. He was carried to the police station, also on Abbey Lane where P.C. Lynch administered 'simple remedies'. It was supposed he had had a fit and would recover so no doctor was sent for. The man was also known to be very nervous in storms. He died several hours later. The jury recorded a verdict of death by natural causes.

The landlord of the inn in December 1890 was Richard Edwards. He was fined forty shillings for allowing drunkenness on the premises. P.C's Keylock and Lynch gave evidence to show there had been a rabbit coursing match on the 22nd November. The inn was very crowded and three men - Joseph Williams, George Powell and Benjamin Davies were charged with being drunk. Williams was fined twenty shillings and the other two ten shillings each.

At Caerleon police court in January 1892, George Barclay, a mason was summoned for being drunk on the 8th. He was found wandering in the yard and gave his excuse as it was only the second time he had been in the place and didn't know his way around. When this excuse failed he claimed his staggering was just the way he was. Police evidence showed he didn't stagger when sober so he was fined five shillings.

Richard Edwards was in court again in 1894 with John Harris. On 18th September Harris had visited the inn after working three shifts with no break. After two pints of cider he fell asleep on the settle. P.S. Lewis found him and woke him up. On doing so he staggered out but not before attempting to drink a glass of beer. Harris's landlady had gone to Newport and so he could not get into his lodgings. He was fined ten shillings. Edwards was fined forty shillings due to previous similar offences.

At Llantarnam Church in May 1895, a disturbing discovery was made. Two men found a man in 'respectable attire' lying on one of the graves. His throat had been cut. He was taken to the Coopers Arms where he revealed he was visiting Llantarnam to go to the grave of his parents and it was there he had been attacked. Dr. Murphy was called and attended to the man's injury. He was later driven to Newport in a 'cab' to the infirmary in critical condition.

On the 1901 census the inn had changed hands again. This time to Thomas Matthews, thirty-seven and wife, 'E.J., thirty-five. They had one son, Bertie aged five and employed a servant, Maud Jones, eighteen.

In May 1902 a porter named Edward Jones, after finishing work at Pontnewydd station was walking the line to Llantarnam when he was hit by a passenger train. It appeared he was walking the wrong side of the line as there was a sharp bend at the scene of the accident and the approaching train could not have been seen. Jones's body was taken to the Coopers Arms to await inquest.

By the time of the 1911 census Edward Thomas was landlord. He was fifty-seven and lived with his wife Clara, forty-eight. They had three children, Hilda, twenty-one, Arthur, fifteen and Edward, eighteen. The census also recorded the inn as having six rooms.

The Coopers Arms closed a few years later. It is said it was bought by Sir Clifford Cory of Llantarnam Abbey because the noise from the inn disturbed his workers. Today it is a private dwelling.

The Greenhouse

The Greenhouse is thought to have been converted from an old grain house once used by the monks of llantarnam Abbey. It became an inn in 1791. A plaque showing two men either side of a table with a candle in the centre drinking from a goblet and a tankard sits above the door. The inscription below them reads -

Y Ty Gwyrdd	The Greenhouse
1719	1719
Cwrw da	Good ale
A seider I chwi	and cider for you
Dewch y mewn	Come in
Chwi gewch y brofi	You shall taste it.

The earliest census, in 1841, shows that Harriet Franks, forty, was the landlady. She lived with her sons, George, fifteen, Charles, thirteen and David, eleven. George was employed as a carpenter and Charles, a gardener.

In September 1849, Caerleon Farmers Club held their annual ploughing match on fields at Pentre Bach Farm. There were also prizes given for the best animals. These were penned in front of the Greenhouse. The Monmouthshire Merlin recorded that 'the quiet little village had scenes of bustle and activity not remembered by the oldest inhabitants'.

Henry Hobbs was landlord on the 1851 census. He was twenty-five and lived with his wife, Mary, twenty-seven. They also employed a maid, Ann Pritchard, sixteen.

Auctions were held at the Greenhouse such as the one in December 1852 where a quantity of live and dead farming stock was removed to the inn for 'convenience of sale'.

An argument over pigs arose in January 1857. Landlord James Thomas had caught and impounded four pigs that had wandered onto his premises from the adjoining farm. The occupier of the farm, Thomas Morris brought court action to see if he had the right to do so. It was also suggested Thomas should pay two pounds to Morris for damage to the pigs which were fat and in good condition before being impounded. Mr Dowling of Llantarnam Abbey was also called to establish whether Morris's pigs had permission to run in a field belonging to the Llantarnam Estate. Both men then referred the whole matter to Mr. Dowling.

The 1861 census took place on 7th April. There was no listing for the Greenhouse and that was because it's entire contents were advertised for sale in the Monmouthshire Merlin of 27th April. Items for sale included long club room tables, carpets, bedroom chairs and beds, long settles, knives and forks, dinner service, set of skittles and bowls, round and square tables, beer trams, a sixty gallon copper boiler, meat saw and cleaver tools, bedsteads with hangings, a malt mill and a coffee mill.

An inquest was held at the inn in August 1869 on the body of John Farrance, a contractor who had been working repairing the church next door. Mr. Brewer was the coroner and he and the jury concluded the death was by natural causes.

A ploughing match was held in October of the same year by Llantarnam Farmers Association. At the end of the competition dinner was served at the Greenhouse by Mr. Evans and presided over by John Lawrence.

The Mr. Evans, was landlord Edward Evans, sixty-five. He was listed on the 1871 census with wife Mary Ann, sixty. With them lived son Henry, twenty-seven, daughter Charlotte, twenty-five, grandson Henry, one and servant Emma Williams, fifteen.

John Jenkins was charged with drunkenness and indecency in May 1873. He was so drunk he was unable to speak. Edward Howells was also charged with being drunk. Sergeant Porall stated he saw them go out of the Greenhouse 'beastly drunk'. They were fined ten shillings plus costs. Richard Evans was charged with permitting drunkenness on his premises. Evans stated the men were drunk before they went in but he did not see their condition before he served them. He was fined three pounds but was surprised thinking he should not have been fined anything.

An extension of opening times was granted to the landlord by the court in September 1882 on the occasion of the annual ploughing match and dinner held on 5th October.

On the 1881 census Edward Evans was still landlord. His son Henry had married Emma and they had four children, Mary, six, Edward, five, Ann, two and Emma, two months. They also employed fourteen year old Emily Richards as a servant.

By June 1887, Henry Evans had become landlord. He was summoned to Caerleon police court at this time for permitting drunkenness at the inn on 31st May. Two police officers visited and found a man, Benjamin Davis, asleep on a settle. When he was woken up he fell down in a drunken heap. Emma Evans said that she had served him but was unaware that he was drunk. Davis was fined ten shillings and Evans paid costs.

The Evans family no longer ran the inn on the 1891 census. Walter Walters, fifty, was landlord. With him was his wife, Elizabeth, forty-six and daughter Lottie, eighteen. There was also a servant Annie Edmunds, twenty.

The annual meeting of Llantarnam Farmers Club was held at Ty Coch farm in October 1892. In the evening their annual dinner was held at the Greenhouse with a large attendance including Colonel Morgan M.P. who presided over proceedings.

In January 1893 Mr Moses Roberts Jones, coroner, held an inquest at the inn into the death of Henry Cartwright, a bottle maker employed at Newport Glass works. Henry was killed at Llantarnam station, possibly from trying to cross the line. The jury returned a verdict of accidental death and recommended the Great Western Railway Company build a bridge across the line for passengers to use.

It was all change again on the 1901 census, The inn was run by Edward Thomas, thirty-nine and wife Mary, thirty-eight. They lived with children – Ivor, six, Daisy, five, William, three and Fred,one. There were two servants – Linda King, sixteen and Florence Edwards, fourteen.

John Power,a labourer from Llantarnam was summoned in January 1892 for being helplessly drunk on a footpath leading from the Greenhouse to the vicarage. He also gave police a false name. He was fined fifteen shillings.

In December 1904, Henry Bartlett, a haulier of Newport was summoned for being so far away from his horse and cart that he had no control over it. He was drinking in the Greenhouse, meanwhile the unattended horse had bolted and was found almost a mile away. He was fined one pound.

Another haulier, Thomas Williams, was summoned by Mrs Susannah Morgan in June 1906 for an assault on her. She said she visited the Greenhouse for her husband. While waiting there Williams approached and without provocation caught hold of her, dragged her along the road and used improper language towards her. He denied the assault but admitted putting his hands on her. He was fined five pounds.

Landlord Edward Thomas was assaulted in July 1906 by two labourers, William Casey and Charles Rabett of Pill and Barrack Hill, Newport. Mr Thomas said that on July 8th a party drove up to his house and someone knocked on the door. They asked for drink but it was after closing time. Without opening the door he told them they were too late. Then someone began kicking the door. Mr Thomas then decided to open it. One of the men caught hold of him and swore at him. Casey said he ought to have his jaw punched. Rabett used similar words. Thomas tried to phone the police but the men assaulted him again. Rabett then offered to fight him for a 'quid' and pushed him which caused him to fall into the road. Both pleaded not guilty but the court fined them two shillings each for the damage to the door and two pounds each for the assault.

Edward Thomas was still landlord at the time of the 1911 census. There was also another child, Charles, born in 1903. Mary Ann Davies, eighteen was employed as a servant.

On the 1939 register the inn was home to Bert Butcher, fifty-one, his wife Maud, fifty and son Kenneth, eighteen.

The Greenhouse has served the community for over three hundred years and is still open today.

Three Blackbirds Inn

The 1841 census shows the three blackbirds in the middle of a group of dwellings simply known as 1 – 6 Two Locks. An 1846 plan of Llantarnam shows Rosser Jenkins as the owner of 'house and garden'.

At number 3 Two Locks lived Joseph Giles, publican, aged sixty. Also there was his wife Elizabeth, fifty, son Joseph, twenty, Thomas, eighteen and daughter Leah, fifteen.

Number 3 Two Locks became known as the Blackbirds Beerhouse on the 1851 census, still occupied by Joseph and Elizabeth Giles. Only one child lived with them at this point, Thomas, who was a carpenter.

By the 1861 census there is only a building known as 'Blackbirds' with one dwelling either side. Joseph Giles, still occupied it. He was a widow living with his son Thomas.

Of the dwellings either side one was occupied Joseph Giles, forty-one, his wife Ann and children Thomas, fifteen, Ann, eleven and Mary, six. The dwelling on the other side occupied by a different family. More evidence that these were individual dwellings comes from the Monmouthshire Merlin of 10th March 1860 where the death of Rachel Watkins, twenty-three, was recorded at her mother's house, 'Blackbirds'

By using the census it looks as though numbers 1 -6 Two Locks became three dwellings known as Blackbirds then finally by the 1871 census the 'Three Blackbirds'. At this time Richard Waite and wife Rachel, both fifty-six, resided there with their daughter Hannah, fourteen.

John Davis, thirty-two, was landlord on the 1881 census. He occupied the premises with wife, Hannah, thirty-five and children Richard, eight and Joseph, two. The family employed a servant, Martha Norman aged seventeen.

James Cox took over the inn sometime during 1883. Also during this year the inn was mentioned in the Monmouthshire Merlin. John Robertson had visited and picked up a whip left behind by a gentleman. He was prosecuted and fined.

In September of the same year James Cox was ordered to pay costs of five shillings and six pence for driving 'furiously' through Commercial Street on a Friday evening. P.S. Brookes stated the four wheels attached to the horse were 'going all over the place'.

James Cox and wife Hannah kept the Blackbirds until 1904. On the 1901 census they were also using the land to farm. They employed a servant, Annie Williams, aged fourteen and also a cow man.

The license of the Three Blackbirds was transferred from James Cox to Albert Matthews in December 1904. This was due to a 'long and painful illness' suffered by Cox which led to his death on February 27th aged 63.

Albert Matthews had vacated the inn by the 1911 census. At this point Joseph Phillips, a fifty-two year old widower lived there with four sons and three daughters. Their names were not recorded only their initials – J.M., son twenty-three, M.G., son twenty-one, J.G. Son, eighteen, R, daughter sixteen, C.M. Daughter fourteen and W, son seven.

The 1939 register records Edward Gillard, forty-seven, living there with wife Winifred, twenty-nine and son Edward, seven.

The tramp poet, W.H. Davies would often end his walks with a visit to a pub and recorded his stop at the Three Blackbirds in 'A Poet's Pilgrimage' in 1918.

'When I reached the Three Blackbirds at Llantarnam I had my first glass of beer of the day and enjoyed it very much. It was a good brew, mild and yet satisfying, frothy and yet without gas. I would most certainly have had a second glass if any company had been present but as I was the only customer it was not long before I left'.

Yew Tree Inn

Yew Tree House was built around 1861 near Ty Coch bridge. Its first occupants were John Matthews, a seventy-three year old shoemaker. On the 1861 census he lived with his wife Margaret, sixty-one and step-daughter, Ann Lewis, twenty.

Ten years later the 1871 census records iron worker Thomas Pattimore, thirty-eight living there with his wife Jane, thirty-six and children – Elizabeth, seven, William, four and Alfred, one.

In November 1873 Mr James Graham was instructed by the trustee of the will of Rees Edward Rees to sell by auction properties within the Ty Coch and Clawd dde estates. This included the Yew Tree inn which had a lease of ninety-nine years from 2nd February 1861. It also included a 'newly built' cottage adjoining the inn.

In August 1890 the landlady of the Yew tree, Mary Jones was recorded in the Free Press as having been fined forty shillings for permitting drunkenness

On 13th August 1890 a sale by auction was held at the Westgate Hotel, Newport. Lot five was the Yew Tree Inn and adjoining cottage. The building was let to Hancock and Co. Brewery and occupied by William Lloyd. The cottage was occupied by Mrs Buns and produced a rental of five pounds. The lot was held under a ninety-nine year lease from 2nd February 1861 at a ground rent of two pounds and ten shillings per annum.

On the 1901 census William Edwards lived at the Yew Tree. He was a forty-four year old puddler. He was not recorded as being a publican. He lived with his wife Sarah, forty-two and children – Harriet, ten, Charley eight, Polly, five, Lillie, four and George, one.

The 1911 census showed Edmund Roberts, sixty, at the inn. Again he was not recorded as being a publican but a boatman. With him was his wife, Mary, fifty-one and step-son Ernest Jones, twenty-one.

The next mention of the Yew Tree was on the 1939 register. Frederick Booth, forty-six, lived there and gave his occupation as that of an iron worker. He lived with his wife Agnes, forty-seven. Also listed was Ralph Booth, seventeen, farm labourer and Clarence Pheasy, forty-six, a builders labourer.

The Yew Tree Inn closed around 1963. The last people to run it were Aggie and Jack Smith. It was turned into a private house. In its walls is a Victorian era post box from when it was used as a post office. It has also been used as a bakery and a shop.

The Wheatsheaf

The location of the Wheatsheaf can be ascertained from an advertisement in the Monmouthshire Merlin of October 1869. It concerned Llantarnam Farmers Association's annual ploughing match. The fields used for ploughing were on Pentre Bach farm in front of the inn.

Nearby was a bridge over the canal named Bullock's Bridge which gives another clue to the inn's location

The earliest recording on the census for the inn is 1841 when John Williams, aged forty was the landlord. He lived with his wife, Elizabeth, thirty and children, Martha, seven and William, one.

On the 1851 census Phillip Bullock, thirty-two lived at the inn with his wife, Sarah, thirty and children – John, ten, Peter, six, Elizabeth, four, Phillip, two and Jacob, one. Phillip's occupation was a boatman. There was also a lodger recorded on the census, William Daniel, also a boatman. The family employed a servant, Elizabeth Williams aged fourteen.

On the 8th March 1856 there was a sale by auction on the premises of furniture belonging to William Williams. Another clue was given as to the Wheatsheaf's location by the Monmouthshire Merlin, that being a quarter of a mile from Llantarnam station. Items for sale included an eight day clock in a mahogany case, a twenty-four hour clock in an oak case, three oak tables and chairs and also farming equipment.

In the Monmouthshire Merlin of 1st February 1866 it was recorded that the license for the Wheatsheaf had been transferred from Jane Herbert to George Bullingham. He occupied the inn on the 1871 census with his wife Mary. They were both seventy years old.

By the time of the 1881 census the Wheatsheaf was run by Mr. W Pritchard and his wife Ann, both sixty-four. They had one son living with them, Joseph, thirty-one.

In October 1889 Ann was a widow and was running the inn herself. In the Pontypool Free Press it was reported that she had been summoned for serving drinks during prohibited hours. P.C. Morgan watched her premises from a spot forty yards away and at 11.50 am saw a number of men drinking there. On going closer he was spotted and the men ran. One man was caught but he gave a false name. Thirteen were counted outside and five inside. Ann told the officer she 'could not help it' but didn't explain why. Superintendent Bosanquet said the house was in a very out of the way location and afforded great facilities for carrying on an illicit trade. The bench took Ann's absence as contempt of court and fined her fifty shillings together with an endorsement of the license.

On the 1891 census the Pritchard family had grown. At the age of seventy-four Ann was still the head of the family. Her son Joseph had married, Mary, thirty-five and had four children – Jacob, eight, Ann, six David, four and Alice, seven months.

Ann had died by 1895 and Joseph took over the running of the inn. In May that year he was prosecuted for selling drink during prohibited hours. On Sunday 12th May at 11 am Officer Keylock found three men in a shed in front of the house, two of which lived in Newport. Each of the men had a pint of beer. Mary Pritchard told the officer she had asked the men where they came from. Joseph said that he was not aware the men were on the premises. Mr. Lyndon Moore, defence solicitor contended the case had not been proved. The bench dismissed the case but ordered the men to pay costs.

The 1901 census gave Joseph Pritchard's occupation as a labourer in the iron works however he was still involved in running the inn. In November of the same year he was charged with opening his house for the sale of drink during prohibited hours. P.S. Norris said that on August 25th at 7.30 am he saw a man named David Beck enter the premises and speak to Joseph. Joseph's daughter then provided him with a pint glass of what looked like beer. Beck paid for it and drank it. Norris then got out of the hedge he had been hiding in and went to the inn. Joseph's daughter said the drink was 'orange champagne' but the glass smelled of beer. The court said the case had been repeatedly adjourned because of an attempt by Beck on his life which caused him to be detained at Newport hospital. Since the summons Beck had also tried to kill himself by cutting his throat. David Beck, a mason said that he had asked the girl for pop and was served two bottles of orange champagne in a pint glass for which he paid four pence. The case was dismissed.

The Pritchards left the Wheatsheaf by October 1902. The new landlord, William Jones was granted an occasional license for the Llantarnam ploughing matches. The same month a vicious attack took place near the inn. Cwmbran colliers, John Jones, Hubert Whitby, Frederick Crockett, John Nichols and Leonard Pike were all charged at Cwmbran police court of stealing a number of articles from Thomas Walters, a tailor from Newport. Walters visited Llantarnam on the afternoon of the 26th and visited the Wheatsheaf for a drink. Here he met the five men who followed him out into the road. On reaching Bullock's Bridge, Walters called them 'fools' for following him. One of the men then threatened to throw him over the bridge and snatched a pipe and stick from him. They all then threw him down and ransacked his pockets. They took three shillings, a wooden pipe, a pocket knife, three pawn tickets and a walking stick. Walters could not identify the men as it was dark on the night in question. The bench dismissed the case due to lack of evidence.

The license for the Wheatsheaf Inn was refused at the Caerleon Brewster sessions in April 1904. It closed its doors on the 5th. The inn was opposed by police as being unnecessary.

The premises was still occupied on the 1911 census but known only as 'Wheatsheaf'. Living there was George Williams, seventy-one who described himself as a pensioner. He lived with his wife, Susan, seventy-five and son Christopher, thirty-four. There was also a grand-daughter, Emma Jones, nineteen.

The building was known as Wheatsheaf Cottage on the 1939 register and was occupied by Christopher Willmott aged 62.

Carpenters Arms

In Ty Coch, in an area called Pentre Basket was the Carpenters Arms. On the 1841 census it was occupied by James Meredith, thirty and his family – Martha, thirty, Joseph, thirteen, Margaret, nine, Mary, seven, Ann, two and William, four months.

On the 1851 census it was home to William Davis, fifty-six and his wife Eliza, thirty-six. They had one daughter living at home, Harriet aged six. Their niece, Eliza Waters, sixteen, was also recorded on the census as was a lodger, William James, thirty-six.

An inquest was held at the inn in June 1859 by W.H. Brewer on the body of George Jones. He had been bathing in the canal but had drowned. A verdict of accidentally drowned was returned.

The next landlord was William Waite. In November 1863 he was charged with having the inn open for the sale of beer on a Sunday morning at 11.15. P.C. 82 proved the case and stated there were four men in the house, one of whom was drunk. A fine of twenty shillings was imposed.

On the 1871 census William Waite was sixty years old and was recorded as being a farmer and a publican. He lived with his wife Catherine, sixty and children – William, a twenty-six year old butcher, Catherine, twenty-two and Eliza, eighteen. There were also two nephews present on census night – Edward, twenty-two and Richard, fourteen. The family also had three lodgers – Thomas Crew, twenty, William Jones, nineteen and Charles Williams, thirty-two.

By the time of the 1881 census, Thomas Bladen, fifty, was the innkeeper. With him was his wife, Hannah, fifty-one and children, Mary, twenty-four, Ellen, eleven, Charles, nine, George, seven and Arthur, three.

By August 1889 the inn had changed hands again. John Evans was landlord. He was also summoned for allowing drunkenness. P.C. Wall visited and found a man named Davies drunk in the kitchen. There were three other men in the house, also drunk including the landlord. On a table was a jug and several glasses of beer. P.C. Wall left and later saw the landlord take Davies across a field and leave him under a hedge. The solicitor defending Evans said the landlord admitted Davies was drunk but it was not him who had served him drink. The police gave the house a very bad character. Evans was fined ten shillings.

John Evans still lived at the Carpenters Arms on the 1891 census. He was forty-six years old and worked both as a labourer and publican. His wife was Mary, forty-eight. They had five children – John, fifteen, Margaret, thirteen, George, eleven, Elizabeth, six and Richard, one.

In August 1901 Mr Lyndon Moore applied for a license for a new premises to be called the Tennis Court Hotel. The license was granted on condition the license for the Carpenters Arms was surrendered.

This, however, did not happen. On the 1901 census the inn was occupied by William Powell, seventy-one and wife Harriet, seventy-two and by the time of the 1911 census it was home to Mary Evans, a sixty-one year old widow who was its landlady. With her was her daughter, Edith, twenty-eight and son Steven, twenty-seven.

The 1911 census provided extra information about the inn, it had seven rooms and its postal address was Carpenters Arms, Baltic, Cwmbran. There was no reference to a Carpenters Arms inn on the 1939 register however there were cottages known as 'Carpenters'.

HENLLYS

Castell-y-Bwch

Translated, the name Castell-y-Bwch means the 'Bucks Castle'. There is no evidence of a castle situated in the area between Llantarnam and Henllys though it may have been possible in years gone by to have seen deer roaming. A Torfaen walks guide gives the sate of the building as 1550 – 1610.

The Castell-y-Bwch was a large farming estate. In February 1840 the Monmouthshire Merlin ran the following advertisement -

'Valuable estates – farmhouse with orchard, two barns, cow house and other outbuildings. Two cottages, blacksmith's shop and several pieces of arable, meadow and pasture land called Castell-y-Bwch'.

A year later in February 1841 the farm was again being advertised as being available to let. At this time it was in the possession of Thomas Roberts. The farmhouse was described as 'substantial' and set in a hundred acres of land plus woodland.

An otter hunt took place in the district in May 1844 with the 'celebrated' dogs of Mr. Lewis of New House, Glamorgan. It was reported in the Monmouthshire Merlin that after a long hunt the party stopped at the Castell-y-Bwch where they 'fought their battles o'er again'.

Later in 1844 the Castell-y-Bwch was advertised in the Monmouthshire Merlin to be sold by auction at the Westgate Inn, Newport on Thursday 12 December at 3 pm. The sale consisted of several pieces of arable, pasture and woodland also a cottage, smith's shop and garden.

At the time of the 1851 census the Castell-y-Bwch was occupied by John Evans, aged forty-five. His occupation was recorded as being a farmer of a hundred acres. He lived with his wife, Elizabeth and children – William, seventeen, Samuel, eleven, John, eight and David, three. There was also Ann Joshua, nineteen, who was employed as a house servant and dairy maid.

The Evans family vacated the Castell-y-Bwch within a couple of years. In June 1854 the Philanthropic Brothers held their anniversary at the Castell-y-Bwch, house of Thomas Edmunds. The Monmouthshire Merlin did not state whether the Castell-y-Bwch was an inn at this point.

Two years later in 1856 the quarterly committee of Oddfellows was held at the Castell-y-Bwch. Under the presidency of Edmund Jones. All eleven lodges in the district were found to be in a prosperous condition with over eleven hundred members.

The next reference to the Castell-y-Bwch appeared on the 1871 census. It was occupied by Benjamin Llewellyn, forty-eight and his wife Sarah, twenty-three. Benjamin's occupation was given as solely an innkeeper. He did not occupy the premises for very long though as by May 1878 the property was advertised in the South Wales Daily News as for sale again. It was described as 'a very compact, freehold property comprising a good dwelling house, out houses, garden and four acres of meadow in the occupation of William Lloyd as tenant'.

Evidence points to the Castell-y-Bwch estate being divided into separate properties. The land it once was set in had shrunk from a hundred acres to four.

In November 1879 the fourth annual meeting of the Henllys Farmers Association was held. Ploughing took place on the land of Mr John Evans, Castle Farm while dinner was held afterwards at the Castell-y-Bwch.

By the 1880s the inn was occupied by Charles Samuel. In March 1882 he was summoned for having his house open at an illegal hour. P.S. Evans said that around 11 pm on the 2nd, he visited and found men and women in the house. Mrs Samuel, who appeared on behalf of her husband, said there had been a concert in the parish that night and once finished some of the people came to the house. The only people supplied with drink were two cab men. The bench decided no offence had been committed but inflicted a fine of twenty shillings to include costs.

At the 1883 licensing sessions in Newport, Sergeant Gurney submitted a list of publicans who had been in breach of the Licensing Act. The Castell-y-Bwch was one of them and so the renewal of its license was opposed.

Mr Evans lived at the farm in the 1880s however on December 1st 1884 many of his items were being sold as he was leaving. Items included live and dead farming stock, six cows, a cart and horses, three pigs, poultry, quantities of oats, wheat and barley, twenty-five tons of swedes, hay, wagons, plough, harrows, pulper and dairy utensils.

The farm may have been vacated but with the inn still open for business Lord Tredegar and hounds met at the inn on 22nd December.

The 1891 census shows how the Castell-y-Bwch estate was divided up into eight separate properties. There were two cottages simply called 'Castell-y-Bwch', Castle Farm, two 'Old Castle' cottages, two inn cottages and the 'Old Castle' itself. Charles Samuel, fifty-seven still occupied the inn with wife Amy, fifty and children, William, thirty-three, Harry, twenty-one, Elizabeth, sixteen, Clara, fourteen, Leah, eleven and Ben, nine.

In 1894 Castell-y-Bwch farm belonged to George Burge, a fishmonger of Newport. In February of that year P.C. Humphries gave Newport magistrates court a report of neglect by John Berry, an elderly man employed by Mr. Burge. The officer found seven horses in one field and eleven in another one. One had died and two were dying. The rest were starving and had eaten the tops off hedges. Further inspection by Inspector Warr of the Royal Society for the Prevention of Cruelty to Animals found no food in the stomach of one of the dead horses. There were pieces of stick and bark in its intestines. Another of the horses was a living skeleton. Mr Burge was partially paralyzed so he had employed Berry to look after the horses and three hundred poultry. There was plenty of food on the farm, the inspector saw eight trusses of hay and twenty bags of barley. When food was eventually given to the horses they were ravenous and kicked each other to get it.

Berry was charged with cruelty though the clerk of the court pointed out there was no overt act of cruelty, just neglect, the onus was on the owner to ensure the horses were fed. The case was adjourned to summon Mr Burge.

Mr Morgan-Phillips, barrister, appeared for Mr Burge. The court heard that Burge was too ill to attend the farm very often but when he did he frequently found Berry in the house smoking while food for the animals remained untouched. He declared he had only just taken the farm and had intended to put up a shed so the horses had shelter. He had since dismissed Berry, an old soldier who had lost his leg in the Crimea.

Mr Burge was fined five pounds even though the court ruled there was no guilty knowledge on his part.

The Samuels family still occupied the inn in 1901. On the census Amy Samuel, sixty, was the landlady. She lived with her four children – Charles, thirty-four, Elizabeth, twenty-six, Clara, twenty-four and Ben, nineteen. The same went for the 1911 census, Amy was still landlady at seventy. Her daughter Elizabeth was married with the surname, Smith. Ben was employed as a mason. Amy's fourteen year old grand-son was also recorded as was the number of rooms at the inn, seven.

We now leave historical evidence and take a detour into the realms of folklore and superstition. In the Weekly Mail of 25th January 1902 was an article written by John Griffith. It explored legends of Wales and the Castell-y-Bwch was mentioned. John Griffith wrote that there was a race of dwarves in Gwent known as the Bwci or sometimes the Pwca and that near to the Castell-y-Bwch stood a house called Ty Pwca. Belief in the Pwca was common in the area. Near to Upper Cwmbran was a farm called Ty Pwca, demolished years ago but there are reminders in modern street names of its location – Heol-y-Pwca, Ty Pwca Place etc. It was believed that if the Pwca or Bwci were called upon for assistance they would help around the house or farm in return for shelter, food and drink. However if mistreated they could become very nasty. Combine these tales of the Pwca with the legends surrounding nearby Twmbarlwm and a race of fairies that resided underground that lured people away never to be seen again and it becomes clear how people centuries ago were fearful of events around them that they didn't understand and blamed it on fairies, witches, the Pwca etc but also respected them. What better way to get on the right side of the Pwca or Bwci by giving them your house – Ty Pwca. Now consider Castell-y-Bwch. What if it never had anything to do with deer but with the Pwca? Not Castell-y-Bwch but Castell-y-Bwci?

Dorallt Inn

Originally there were two farms adjacent to each other, the Dorallt Fawr and the Dorallt Fach. It is the Dorallt Fawr that became an inn, the Cwrt Henllys Hotel is on the site of the Dorallt Fach.

The 1851 census showed the Dorallt Fawr was a farm of thirty-nine acres. Occupying it was Richard Saunders, thirty-nine and his wife, Eliza, thirty-seven. They had six children – Eliza, twenty-one, John, thirteen, Richard, nine, Sarah, seven, Phillip, three and William, four months.

The Dorallt Fawr remained a farm for the next few years. The 1871 census showed the son of Richard Saunders, also Richard lived at the Dorallt Fach. He had two occupations that of a farmer and a miner. The Dorallt Fawr was occupied by Richard Williams and wife, Jane.

It was at this point the Dorallt Fawr was recorded as being an inn, for in the County Observer of 29th July 1871 a report stated that W.H. Brewer, coroner, held an inquest at the inn on the body of Richard Jenkins who had died from a fit on the 20th.

The 1881 census classed the Dorallt Fawr as both a farm and an inn occupied by Thomas Howells however the following year it was up for sale. The Monmouthshire Merlin gave a description of the sale. The Dorallt was a double licensed public house, near the coal works doing a good trade. There was now only eighteen acres of land, mostly pasture, some arable and some orchard. Also for sale was its barn, cow house, piggeries and stable.

The landlord of the Dorallt in November 1890 was George Allen. He was recorded in the South Wales Echo as being summoned to Newport county police court along with William Evans for being drunk on licensed premises and for permitting drunkenness. At 9.45 pm, on 11th October, P.C. Harris and another officer visited the Dorallt and found Evans drunk in the passage and Allen 'queer' inside a room. Two men later came for beer but Allen said 'You will have no beer – the policeman says we are all drunk'. Afterwards, Evans fought with his two sons in the road and gave the officers about an hour's work to separate them. The bench fined them both ten shillings plus costs in Allen's case.

On the 1891 census the Dorallt was recorded as being an inn only. The landlord was James Roberts, fifty-four. He lived with his wife Harriet, forty-three and their eight children – Magdalene, sixteen, Sarah, fourteen,

Tom, twelve, Edith, eleven, Arthur, eight, Annie, six, Bessie, three and Fred nine months.

James Roberts was described in the Pontypool Free Press as being a 'fine specimen of a host of a village inn' He was in court because James Marsh, a collier had been summoned for being drunk and refusing to leave the inn. Roberts said that Marsh had come in drunk and was served but as soon as he realised he stopped tap on him and ordered him to leave. Marsh refused to go and as there was no one to remove him he stayed until closing time. Marsh said it was 'all over the election'. He said he never drank and was very sorry. He was fined five shillings.

The dark lonely roads around the Dorallt could be a dangerous place. In July 1863 widow Jane Andrews, fifty, of Castell-y-Bwch had been at the inn helping her sister move some furniture. It was late at night when she set off home. As she walked a young farm labourer, Thomas Evans, sprang out from the side of the road and attacked her, knocking her down and attempting to 'criminally assault her'. The South Wales Echo reported that she tore his collar and tie off and screamed 'murder!' several times. A woman named Jane Saunders and a Mrs Collins living in cottages nearby heard her cries and though both were in bed they quickly got dressed and went to her assistance. Mrs Saunders arrived first and found the attack was still in progress. She tried to pull Evans off Jane who was exhausted. Her bonnet had gone, her shawl was torn to pieces and her arms covered in bruises. Mrs Collins took her to her home where she stayed the night.

Officer Keylock arrested Evans. The newspaper almost tried to excuse his behaviour by writing 'It should be stated that he was in drink at the time'. The magistrates remanded him in custody on the charge of 'attempting to ravish a woman old enough to be his mother'.

Mrs Andrews remained hysterical all night after the attack. Evans stated he was so drunk he recalled nothing however he did plead guilty. Mr Gardner, defending him pleaded for a lenient sentence. The bench sent him to prison for two months for aggravated assault.

The owner of the Dorallt in September 1898 was William Thomas. He was advertising to let the property – a fully licensed house plus twenty acres of land – in the Evening Express.

The Dorallt had changed hands again by the time of the 1901 census. Edward Stephens, forty-seven, was the landlord living with wife, Leah, forty-five, daughters, Rhoda, seventeen, Janet, fifteen and sons Edgar, eleven and Brinley, three.

Tragedy struck the Stephens family in March 1906. While at work in Cwmbran Colliery Edward Stephens was buried under a huge fall of roof. Other miners rushed to his aid but another roof fall sent them running for their lives. As soon as the roof was made safe another rescue attempt was made and his body was recovered having been dead for some time. His body was taken to the Dorallt. His son, sixteen, was also badly injured in the same fall.

It was all change again on the 1911 census. William Thomas, thirty-nine, was landlord living with wife, Mary Jane, thirty-nine and children John, ten, Phyllis, six, Gwynneth, three and Gwladys, two.

The Miners Arms

Situated in Bellevue Terrace, Henllys, the Miners Arms was not actually a public house but an off-license. Alcohol was not supposed to be consumed on the premises

In August 1893 the property was sold by auction and described as an 'off-license house and extensive premises' It was auctioned along with the adjoining house and garden occupied by George Marsh.

The next recorded person at the Miners Arms was Alfred John Smith. In July 1896 he was summoned for allowing drinking on his premises. P.C. Bird found four men sitting on a bank about four yards from the front door. Smith said he had served them only one jug of beer which was two-thirds full. One of the men said Smith should pull down his sign if he couldn't sell beer. Smith's defence was that he had no idea where the beer was going to be consumed once it had left his premises. John Williams, a miner who lived close by gave evidence that he went for a 'supper beer' and met three friends. He then bought a jug of beer, the jug having been brought from his own home and had no intention of drinking it in the road. The bench dismissed the case but told Smith to be careful as he had been convicted of a similar offence the previous May.

Smith was summoned again in December 1897 for selling drink and allowing it to be drunk on his premises. One Saturday afternoon P.S. Humphries and P.C. Evans saw several colliers from the adjacent mine drinking there. Mr. Lyndon Moore for the defence said the miners went there to pay their two week drinks bill and were given beer as a discount in hand. The bench stated that no one should be drinking on the premises and that it was illegal. Smith was fined twenty shillings.

In March 1901 at Newport county police court an application was made by John Walters for a full transfer of the Miners Arms. Superintendent Porter opposed on the grounds that the only person in residence at the property was a young girl of sixteen. John Walters was living on a farm elsewhere in the neighbourhood. The bench adjourned while Walters moved in to the house.

Four months later Walters was summoned under Section 5 of the Act of 1872 for allowing beer to be consumed on the highway near his premises. It was Sunday June 16th when P.S. Humphreys and P.C. Bale were watching the house. They saw men go in and come back out wiping their mouths. About 1 pm they saw a group of ten men, twelve yards from the house drinking from jugs which were re-filled several times. The landlord received six pence in payment. When approached he said 'I did not think I was doing any harm, I have done the same thing ever since I have been here and I have drank gallons of beer here myself before I kept the house'. For the defence Mr. Parsons called witnesses to show the landlord took no part in the activities outside of the house and that the men brought their own jugs and bottles. The bench found an offence had been committed, aggravated by the bad character of the house and that the landlord had taken no notice when warned of it. He was fined five pounds.

Walters did not stay at the Miners Arms for very long after that and in September 1901 the license was granted to George Bishop. At the Brewster sessions, twenty-two years of military service went in his favour plus he had managed a public house for four years. The chairman hoped Bishop would do well and find a way to supply 'non-intoxicants' as well as intoxicants and find it profitable. He also added Bishop was not to put 'whiskey in the tea'.

In March 1904 George Bishop was summoned for opening his house during prohibited hours on Saturday February 27th at 10.45 pm and also for selling beer that was being consumed on the premises. P.S. Smith and P.C. Campbell saw two men, John Ellis and William Jones go into the house by the side door without knocking. Five minutes later they entered and found the two men with the landlord at the bar. The landlord was behind the counter and the men in front with beer in front of them. The landlord said the bottles had been paid for a long time ago and that he had given the men the beer, free. The men though denied owning the bottles. For the defence, the landlord said because he was giving up the house the two men had called to see about buying some ducks. The bench fined Bishop five pounds. The two men were fined ten shillings each and the license was transferred from Bishop to William Jones.

William Jones did not stay at the Miners Arms very long either and the license must have been scrapped not long after. By the time of the 1911 census William Samuel was living there with his wife Mary, forty-four and children, Maud, eighteen, Fred, ten, Mabel, seven, Amy, five, and Leslie, three. The census recorded the premises had eight rooms. William Samuel's occupation did not involve retail of any kind, he was a collier.

UPPER CWMBRAN

The Squirrel Inn

The Square in Upper Cwmbran was built around the 1840's. It was seen on the tithe map of 1840 but not on an estate map of 1834. The houses were built for workers in the nearby coal mine and brick works. Here was situated the Squirrel Inn. It was advertised as a business letting in 1845.

'The Squirrel Inn at Cwmbrane adjoining the Porthmawr Coal Works and Firebrick Works of the Stourbridge Clay Company. These works are daily increasing in magnitude and importance and the inn is so situated as to command the custom of he greater part of the population'.

The Monmouthshire Merlin recorded the increasing prosperity of the oddfellowship of Cwmbran in July 1850 whose lodge was at the Squirrel Inn. Almost two hundred attended their anniversary which included a meal provided by host Mrs Prosser. Songs were later sung and toasts given to Thomas Prosser and his wife.

An inquest was held at the inn in July 1853. The landlord at the time was Mr. Edmunds. Mr. Brewer performed the inquest on the body of Morris Stevens aged one year and five months. He was the son of a collier who lived on the side of the mountain. On 21st July his mother went out leaving the children in the care of the eldest daughter who was just ten years old. She heard Morris screaming and on returning found him in flames. He was severely burned and died the next day. A verdict of accidental death was given.

By this time an upstairs room of the inn was being used as a school. David Morgan was the head teacher and managed it for fourteen years. He kept a diary of day to day life in the school, from the noise of the customers in the inn below to truancy and boys working in the mine instead of attending lessons. Hygiene was also an issue due to overcrowding. The school closed in 1868 and a more suitable premises built.

The twelfth anniversary of the Good Intent Lodge of Oddfellows took place on Monday 25th August. The lodge room of the inn was decorated with flowers and evergreens. About 10 pm the company separated after speeches and songs. Dancing then began and continued until dawn.

The following year the lodge celebrated at the inn again. Around ninety-seven members met at 10 am to attend Elim Chapel. On their return they were provided with dinner by landlord John Borwell. At ten that night the room was cleaned for the annual ball for wives and girlfriends who danced to the music of Mr. Powell of Abergavenny until the early hours.

In March 1857 a notice was published in the Monmouthshire Merlin by

Mark Edwards, engine driver of Upper Cwmbran. His wife Caroline had 'absconded' and taken with her a box and other valuables. He stated in the notice he would not be responsible for any debts accrued by her. There was a reward offered to any person who could provide George Thomas of the Squirrel Inn with any information leading to the recovery of the box.

The Spring Hope Philanthropic Order held their fourth anniversary at the inn in August 1858. After lodge business they formed a procession to attend chapel.

An inquest was held at the inn in December 1858 by W. H. Brewer concerning James Hudd, twenty-two who worked as a miner in number 2 level Cwmbran. A fall of rubbish fractured his skull. A verdict of accidental death was recorded.

In October 1859 landlord George Thomas decided to leave the inn. He advertised in the Monmouthshire Merlin of 29th October -

'To be let and entered immediately the old established Squirrel Inn'. Income was described as moderate with two good clubs connected with the house. George also stated he could give good reasons as to why he was leaving.

The Squirrel Inn does not appear to be listed on the 1861 census, maybe a tenant couldn't be found but the school continued there until 1868. The inn survived into the twentieth century but was in ruins by the 1960's and nothing remains of it today.

The Crown Inn

On the 1851 census, on the enumerators route, the Crown Inn was placed between Mountain Cottage and Mountain Farm. At this time it was occupied by Eliza Jenkins, a widow at thirty-eight. She employed a servant, Mary Williams aged nineteen.

In February 1856 an inquest was held at the inn by W. Brewer on the body of William Watkins. He had been kicked by a horse and died from his injuries. Mr. Green, a mineral agent stated that Watkins had not considered the horse to be dangerous. The jury returned a verdict of accidental death.

Charles Evans, forty, occupied the property on the 1861 census. He may not have been a publican as he gives his occupation as coal merchant. He lived with his wife, Rhoda and children - Albert, eight and Emma, two.

On the 1871 census the inn is known as the Crown Tavern. It was occupied by Henry Edwards, sixty-six and wife Elizabeth, thirty-nine. Mary Lloyd, Henry's niece also lived there.

The next landlord was John Jenkins. He was thirty on the 1881 census. He lived with his wife, Rachel, twenty-nine and son Augustus, one.

In October 1885 John Jenkins was charged with being drunk in his own pub. P.C. Williams stated he had visited on 19th September and in the front kitchen found Jenkins leaning across a table in a drunken manner. On being questioned, Jenkins replied 'I have had a drop but I hope you will look over it this time'. He then tried to stand up but he was so drunk he had to hold on to two tables to steady himself. However, witnesses gave evidence that said Jenkins was perfectly sober at the time of the policeman's visit. William Price, a barber said Jenkins had come to his shop at 8 pm for his usual shave. Mr Price's neighbour said she saw Jenkins after he left the barber and he was sober. Jabez Rogers, a labourer, said he was in the Crown when the policeman was there and said Jenkins was carrying on his business in a normal manner and appeared sober. Zephaniah Williams was also in the Crown and said words to the same effect. The magistrates gave Jenkins the benefit of the doubt and dismissed the case.

John Jenkins had died by the time of the 1891 census. His wife Rachel had married Edwin Pool. Augustus Jenkins still lived with them plus they had another son, Harold Pool, three and daughter Elsie Pool, three.

The next mention of the Crown was in the Evening Express of 13th November 1909 when Moses Moreton, a collier, was fined forty shillings for being drunk and refusing to leave the inn on October 29th.

On the 1911 census it was recorded the Crown had seven rooms and was home to William Williams and his wife Gertrude, twenty-six. They had two children – Gwenllian, three and Madge, one.

The Crown Inn building was listed on the 1939 register when William T Berry, a labourer lived there. He was thirty-two and lived with Alice Berry, forty-five but it is no longer around today.

The Bush Inn

On Saturday 12th August 1848 at 3 o clock in the afternoon at the King's Head, Newport, the Bush Inn was sold by auction. As well as the inn, stables, a pigs cot and gardens were included. At this time the occupier was John Thomas. The building was leased for a term of twenty-one years beginning on 1st January 1840.

When the 1851 census was taken, Thomas Prosser was landlord. He was thirty-six and lived with his wife Leah, thirty-two and children - Thomas, nine, Susannah, four, Roger, two and Frederick, one.

The same year, on 5th May, The Bush was sold by auction at the Westgate Hotel, Newport. In this sale there was also an adjoining cottage. The rent paid by Thomas Prosser was forty pounds per year and the inn was leased by William Williams.

Community events were held at the Bush. The Spring Hope Lodge celebrated their anniversary there in August 1856. Around seventy members sat down to a dinner after business was attended to.

By the time of the 1861 census Elizabeth Jones was landlady. In December of that year she was charged with keeping her house open during prohibited hours. P.C. 87 said he had stopped by the Bush after midnight and found twelve men in there drinking beer. She was fined twelve shillings.

The next known landlord was Thomas Edmunds. He was landlord until 12th May 1866 when he died of consumption aged fifty-five. The Monmouthshire Merlin reported that he was much respected and his death was deeply regretted by all who knew him.

At the Bush on Christmas Eve 1866, a presentation was given to Mr and Mrs Joseph Green who for sixteen years had been a mineral agent to John Lawrence. The presentation took place in the largest room however it seemed all of Cwmbran attended and the room was too small. Many speeches were given along with toasts to the prosperity of Cwmbran. The evening ended with singing.

On the 1871 census Charles Samuel, thirty-six, was landlord. With him lived his wife Anne, thirty-six and children – William, thirteen, Anne, seven, Charles, four and Henry,one.

An inquest was held at the inn in October 1871 on the body of John Witney aged twenty years. He was a labourer who had offered to show the dray-men of Commercial Brewery, Newport a byway by which they would avoid paying turnpike tolls. As they went along the road though their cart overturned and he was thrown under it. He called out to the dray-men – 'Help me I am hurt' but after that never spoke again. When help arrived it was found he had broken his neck. A verdict of accidental death was recorded.

The next mention of the Bush was in the County Observer of August 1881 when John Thomas and Thomas Edwards were summoned for being drunk at the inn. The were fined ten shillings each. Then in October 1881 the Cambrian newspaper published a list of bankruptcies of which Benjamin Jenkins, landlord of the Bush was one.

A fete was held in Upper Cwmbran on Monday 7th July 1890. There were prizes for races, hurdles, high jumps, long jumps, donkey racing, sack racing and three legged racing. The entry fee was one shilling and all enquiries had to be given to W. Morgan, secretary, of the Bush Inn.

On the 1891 census Elizabeth Jenkins, forty-two, was landlady. She lived with her children – Arthur, twelve, Ernest, eleven, Anne, five, Lizzie, five and Dan,two. Also there was her mother, Elizabeth Thomas, seventy-five, brother John Morgan, forty-seven and a lodger, William Lewis,forty.

The South Wales Colliers Federation held their monthly meeting at the inn on February 1892. Thomas Richards, a miners agent, presided and a lodge that was recently started at Henllys was admitted to the district.

In February 1895 a gathering took place, the reason being to present Dr.

Campbell with a testimonial. He was assistant to Dr. C. S. Booker. The testimonial was from employees and officials at the Patent Nut and Bolt Factory and took the form of a case of surgical instruments.

Upper Cwmbran Burial Club held a meeting in December 1900. George Jones presided and the auditors were pleased to report the death toll for the year was not as many as the previous year. The number for 1900 being eight.

On the 1901 census, George Short, fifty-seven, was landlord. He lived at the inn with wife Jane, fifty-eight and daughter Ethel, fourteen.

Ten years later the Bush had changed hands again. William Williams, sixty, was landlord. He lived with wife, Lucy, fifty-eight, son Llewellyn, seventeen, daughter, Edith Powell, twenty and son-in-law Henry Powell,twenty-five.

The Bush Inn was recorded on the 1939 register. Landlord Thomas Moreton, sixty-six, though was recorded as being retired. At the property was also Mary Moreton, forty-seven, George Wood, seventy-six and retired and Florence Sillert, forty-four, a widow.

The Queen Inn

Built in the mid 1840s the Queen's first mention in the records was on the 1861 census. Charles Samuel, twenty-six, lived there but gave his occupation as a miner. He lived with his wife Amy, twenty-one and children – William, three and Florence, one. They also employed a servant, Martha Sheen aged twelve.

In September 1861 Charles Samuel was charged with keeping the inn open during prohibited hours. P.C. Watkins stated that he visited there on Monday 9th September just after ten o clock at night and found it full of men. Plus there were many more at the next house as there was not room for them all to fit in the inn. The reason for the large gathering was a supper being held. P.C. Watkins told Mrs Samuel she would be fined. Her reply was that she would 'make the most of it'. They were fined two pounds and nine shillings.

By the 1871 census the inn was run by the Moreton family who kept it for many years. Rachel Moreton, thirty-two, was landlady. She lived with children – Sarah, eleven, Amy, eight, Charles, four and Edward, one. At this time it was known as the Queen Tavern.

On the 1881 census Mary A Moreton was landlady. She was an unmarried eighteen year old at the time and lived with a large family consisting of sister, Matilda, twelve, Aunt Amariah Moreton, thirty-two, nephews Charles, fifteen, Edward, twelve, Moses, seven and Stanley, two. There were also two nieces – Agnes, six and Eveline, five. A servant was also employed – Elizabeth Linney, twenty-one.

In 1890 Thomas Moreton held the license to the Queen Inn. He had actually held it since 1877 but lived elsewhere in Upper Cwmbran while other family members did the job of running it. In September of 1890 he was charged with permitting drunkenness. P.C. Jones stated that he visited the inn and in the front room he found two men named White and Jones drinking beer. The landlord's attention was drawn who then threw them out. P.C. Jones also found nine other men in the house. The defence said the landlord did not realise the men were drunk and had a clear record. The case was dismissed.

The following month the license for the inn was up for renewal. At police court M. Phillips appeared in support of Thomas Moreton. Police had rejected the application for a new license owing to disorderly conduct at the house plus the fact Thomas Moreton did not live on the premises. However Mr Phillips added that he had taken up residence there and would remain there. As to his character he offered to produce a list of a hundred and sixteen households from Upper Cwmbran who would support his fitness to hold a license. It was also pointed out that during a period of forty-five years the inn had been with the Moreton family. Superintendent James was worried about the amount of drunkenness but granted the license.

On the 1891 census William Jones, twenty-six, and his wife Matilda (Moreton), twenty-two were running the inn. They had two children – Lilley, three and Thomas, one.

Thomas Moreton was still the license holder and on 1st June 1891 he was charged with permitting drunkenness. Thomas Hickman and Leonard Johnson were charged with being drunk. All were fined ten shillings each. There was no endorsement on the license due to the previous good character of the inn.

On the 17th June in the South Wales Echo, brewery Phillips and sons advertised the Queen beer house to be let. Later that year, in September at the brewster sessions in Pontypool the police served notice of objection to the renewal of the Queen's license.

A report in the Pontypool Free Press gives an insight into the quite dangerous area that surrounded the Queen. At a meeting of the Llanfrechfa Upper Local Board in April 1892 a surveyors report recorded a new drain put near the inn but part of the embankment close by had slipped down onto the road which had to be removed. There was also no fence around a brook to prevent anything falling in it. A letter had been sent to to the landowner Mr R G Roberts but there had been no reply.

The 1901 census recorded Thomas Moreton, sixty-nine living at the Queen's with his wife Mary Ann, seventy-one. There were no other family members living there and Thomas's occupation was a miner suggesting that the inn was not licensed to sell alcohol but was being used as a dwelling. It was definitely licensed by the 1911 census though. It had been taken over by John Williams, forty-eight, who gave his occupation as both a miner and a licensed victualler. He lived with his wife Mary, forty-four and children – Lily, eighteen and Stanley, sixteen and also a nephew, William Griffiths, twenty-seven.

The next available register of 1939 showed Henry and Mary Byard, both forty-seven occupying the premises along with daughter Mary, fifteen. The Queen Inn remains open to this day.

PHOTOS

WATERLOO INN

PONTNEWYDD INN

YEW TREE INN

OAKFIELD INN

THE GREENHOUSE

THE HALFWAY HOTEL
(MIDDLE RIGHT)

RAILWAY INN

THE MOON INN

ODDFELLOWS
(MIDDLE RIGHT)

NEW BRIDGEND INN

THE
ABB
EY
HOT
EL

REFERENCES

Monmouthshire Merlin
Pontypool Free Press
Pontypool Messenger
UK Census Collection 1840 – 1911
1939 Register
Evening Express
County Observer
Cardiff Times
South Wales Echo
South Wales Daily News
Western Mail
Illustrated Usk Observer
1901 Kelly's Directory
Welsh Tithe Maps
The Cambrian
A   Poets   Pilgrimage   –   W   H   Davies

ABOUT THE AUTHOR

Carol Ann Lewis was born in South Wales in 1969. She attended Llantarnam School, Cwmbran where she had poetry lessons with Gillian Clarke. She wrote local history articles for the Co-Star newsletter that was distributed around Cwmbran. In 2002 she was a winner in a poetry competition judged by Patrick Jones, brother of Nicky Wire of the Manic Street Preachers. Her first novel Hanbury Park was published in 2013 and she has also written a number of local history books. She graduated from the University of South Wales in 2015 after studying the history of Wales. She was secretary of Cwmbran Writers Group until 2016. She has four children and eight grand-children.

Printed in Great Britain
by Amazon